Kerry Young, Dan Evans and Ron Holt

ESSENTIALS

AQA
GCSE Science A
evision Guide

Contents

Contents

N.B. The numbers in brackets correspond to the reference numbers on the AQA GCSE Science A specification.

How Science Works Overview

How Science Works – Explanation

The AQA GCSE Science specification incorporates:

- **Science Content** – all the scientific explanations and evidence that you need to know for the exams. (It is covered on pages 12–69 of this revision guide.)
- **How Science Works** – a set of key concepts, relevant to all areas of science. It covers...
  - the relationship between scientific evidence, and scientific explanations and theories
  - how scientific evidence is collected
  - how reliable and valid scientific evidence is
  - the role of science in society
  - the impact science has on our lives
  - how decisions are made about the ways science and technology are used in different situations, and the factors affecting these decisions.

Your teacher(s) will have taught these two types of content together in your science lessons. Likewise, the questions on your exam papers will probably combine elements from both types of content. So, to answer them, you'll need to recall and apply the relevant scientific facts and knowledge of how science works.

The key concepts of How Science Works are summarised in this section of the revision guide (pages 5–11). You should be familiar with all of these concepts. If there is anything you are unsure about, ask your teacher to explain it to you.

How Science Works is designed to help you learn about and understand the practical side of science. It aims to help you develop your skills when it comes to...

- evaluating information
- developing arguments
- drawing conclusions.

The Thinking Behind Science

Science attempts to explain the world we live in.

Scientists carry out investigations and collect evidence in order to...

- **explain phenomena** (i.e. how and why things happen)
- **solve problems** using evidence.

Scientific knowledge and understanding can lead to the **development of new technologies** (e.g. in medicine and industry), which have a huge impact on **society** and the **environment**.

The Purpose of Evidence

Scientific evidence provides **facts** that help to answer a specific question and either **support** or **disprove** an idea or theory. Evidence is often based on data that has been collected through **observations** and **measurements**.

To allow scientists to reach conclusions, evidence must be...

- **repeatable** – other people should be able to repeat the same process
- **reproducible** – other people should be able to reproduce the same results
- **valid** – it must be repeatable, reproducible and answer the question.

N.B. If data isn't repeatable and reproducible, it can't be valid.

To ensure scientific evidence is repeatable, reproducible and valid, scientists look at ideas relating to...

- observations
- investigations
- measurements
- data presentation
- conclusions and evaluation.

How Science Works Overview

Observations

Most scientific investigations begin with an **observation**. A scientist observes an event or phenomenon and decides to find out more about how and why it happens.

The first step is to develop a **hypothesis**, which suggests an explanation for the phenomenon. Hypotheses normally suggest a relationship between two or more **variables** (factors that change).

Hypotheses are based on…
- careful observations
- existing scientific knowledge
- some creative thinking.

The hypothesis is used to make a **prediction**, which can be tested through scientific investigation. The data collected from the investigation will…
- support the hypothesis **or**
- show it to be untrue (refute it) **or**
- lead to the modification of the original hypothesis or the development of a new hypothesis.

If the hypothesis and models we have available to us do not completely match our data or observations, we need to check the validity of our observations or data, or amend the models.

Sometimes, if the new observations and data are valid, existing theories and explanations have to be revised or amended, and so scientific knowledge grows and develops.

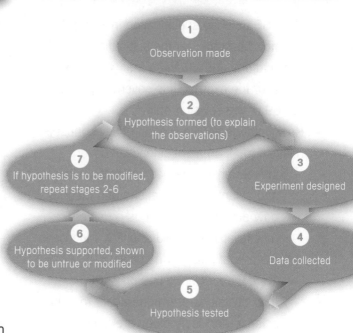

1. Observation made
2. Hypothesis formed (to explain the observations)
3. Experiment designed
4. Data collected
5. Hypothesis tested
6. Hypothesis supported, shown to be untrue or modified
7. If hypothesis is to be modified, repeat stages 2-6

Example

- Two scientists **observe** that freshwater shrimp are only found in certain parts of a stream.
- They use scientific knowledge of shrimp and water flow to develop a **hypothesis**, which relates the presence of shrimp (dependent variable) to the rate of water flow (independent variable). For example, a hypothesis could be: the faster the water flows, the fewer shrimp are found.
- They **predict** that shrimp are only found in parts of the stream where the water flow rate is below a certain value.
- They **investigate** by counting and recording the number of shrimp in different parts of the stream, where water flow rates differ.
- The **data** shows that more shrimp are present in parts of the stream where the flow rate is below a certain value. So, the data **supports** the hypothesis. But, it also shows that shrimp aren't always present in these parts of the stream.
- The scientists realise there must be another factor affecting the distribution of shrimp. They **refine their hypothesis**.

Investigations

An **investigation** involves collecting data to find out whether there is a relationship between two **variables**. A variable is a factor that can take different values.

In an investigation there are two types of variables:
- **Independent** variable – can be changed by the person carrying out the investigation. For example, the amount of water a plant receives.
- **Dependent** variable – measured each time a change is made to the independent variable, to see if it also changes. For example, the growth of the plant (measured by recording the number of leaves).

For a measurement to be valid it must measure only the appropriate variable.

Variables can have different types of values:
- **Continuous variables** – can take any numerical value (including decimals). These are usually measurements, e.g. temperature.
- **Categoric variables** – a variable described by a label, usually a word, e.g. different breeds of dog or blood group.
  - **Discrete variables** – only take whole-number values. These are usually quantities, e.g. the number of shrimp in a stream.
  - **Ordered variables** – have relative values, e.g. 'small', 'medium' or 'large'.

N.B. Numerical values, such as continuous variables, tend to be more informative than ordered and categoric variables.

An investigation tries to find out whether an **observed** link between two variables is…
- **causal** – a change in one variable causes a change in the other, e.g. the more cigarettes you smoke, the greater the chance that you will develop lung cancer.
- **due to association** – the changes in the two variables are linked by a third variable, e.g. as grassland decreases, the number of predators decreases (caused by a third variable, i.e. the number of prey decreasing).
- **due to chance** – the change in the two variables is unrelated; it is coincidental, e.g. people who eat more cheese than others watch more television.

Controlling Variables

In a **fair test**, the only factor that should affect the dependent variable is the independent variable. Other **outside variables** that could influence the results are kept the same, i.e. constant (control variables) or eliminated.

It's a lot easier to control all the other variables in a laboratory than in the field, where conditions can't always be controlled. The impact of an outside variable (e.g. light intensity or rainfall) has to be reduced by ensuring all the measurements are affected by it in the same way. For example, all the measurements should be taken at the same time of day.

Control groups are often used in biological and medical research to make sure that any observed results are due to changes in the independent variable only.

A sample is chosen that 'matches' the test group as closely as possible except for the variable that is being investigated, e.g. testing the effect of a drug on reducing blood pressure. The control group must be the same age, gender, have similar diets, lifestyles, blood pressure, general health, etc.

How Science Works Overview

Investigations (Cont.)

Accuracy and Precision

How accurate data needs to be depends on what the investigation is trying to find out. For example, when measuring the volume of acid needed to neutralise an alkaline solution it is important that equipment is used that is able to accurately measure volumes of liquids.

The data collected must be **precise** enough to form a **valid conclusion**: it should provide clear evidence for or against the hypothesis.

Measurements

Apart from control variables, there are a number of factors that can affect the reliability and validity of measurements:

- **Accuracy of instruments** – depends on how accurately the instrument has been calibrated. An accurate measurement is one that is close to the true value.
- **Resolution (or sensitivity) of instruments** – determined by the smallest change in value that the instrument can detect. The more sensitive the instrument, the more **precise** the value. For example, bathroom scales aren't sensitive enough to detect changes in a baby's mass, but the scales used by a midwife are.
- **Human error** – even if an instrument is used correctly, human error can produce random differences in repeated readings or a systematic shift from the true value if you lose concentration or make the same mistake repeatedly.
- **Systematic error** – can result from repeatedly carrying out the process incorrectly, making the same mistake each time.
- **Random error** – can result from carrying out a process incorrectly on odd occasions or by fluctuations in a reading. The smaller the random error the greater the accuracy of the reading.

To ensure data is as accurate as possible, you can…

- calculate the **mean** (average) of a set of repeated measurements to reduce the effect of random errors
- increase the number of measurements taken to improve the reliability of the mean / spot anomalies.

Preliminary Investigations

A trial run of an investigation will help identify appropriate values to be recorded, such as the number of repeated readings needed and their range and interval.

You need to examine any **anomalous** (irregular) values to try to determine why they appear. If they have been caused by equipment failure or human error, it is common practice to ignore them and not use them in any calculations.

There will always be some variation in the actual value of a variable, no matter how hard we try to repeat an event.

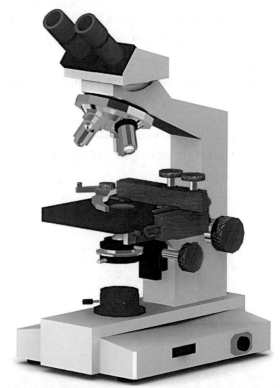

Presenting Data

Data is often presented in a **chart** or **graph** because it makes…

- any patterns more obvious
- it easier to see the relationship between two variables.

The **mean** (or average) of data is calculated by adding all the measurements together, then dividing by the number of measurements taken:

$$\text{Mean} = \frac{\text{Sum of all Values}}{\text{Number of Values}}$$

If you present data clearly, it is easier to identify any anomalous (irregular) values. The type of chart or graph you use to present data depends on the type of variable involved:

1 **Tables** organise data (but patterns and anomalies aren't always obvious)

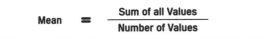

Height of student (cm)	127	165	149	147	155	161	154	138	145
Shoe size	5	8	5	6	5	5	6	4	5

2 **Bar charts** display data when the independent variable is categoric or discrete and the dependent variable is continuous.

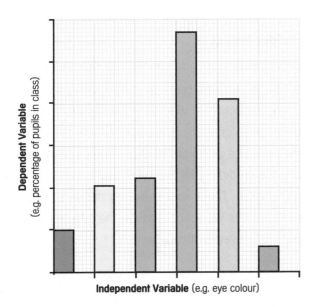

Dependent Variable (e.g. percentage of pupils in class)

Independent Variable (e.g. eye colour)

3 **Line graphs** display data when both variables are continuous.

- Points are joined by straight lines if you don't have data to support the values between the points.
- A line of best fit is drawn if there is sufficient data or if a trend can be assumed.

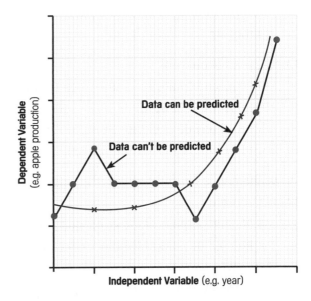

Dependent Variable (e.g. apple production)

Data can be predicted

Data can't be predicted

Independent Variable (e.g. year)

4 **Scattergrams** (scatter diagrams) show the underlying relationship between two variables. This can be made clearer if you include a **line of best fit**. A line of best fit could be a straight line or a smooth curve.

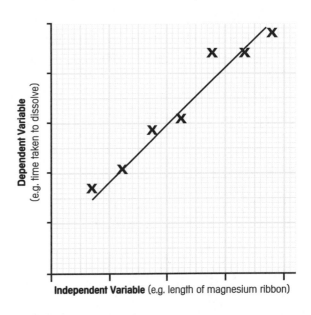

Dependent Variable (e.g. time taken to dissolve)

Independent Variable (e.g. length of magnesium ribbon)

How Science Works Overview

Conclusions **should**…

- describe patterns and relationships between variables
- take all the data into account
- make direct reference to the original hypothesis or prediction
- try to explain the results / observations by making reference to the hypothesis as appropriate.

Conclusions **should not**…

- be influenced by anything other than the data collected (i.e. be biased)
- disregard any data (except anomalous values)
- include any unreasoned speculation.

An **evaluation** looks at the whole investigation. It should consider…

- the original purpose of the investigation
- the appropriateness of the methods and techniques used
- the reliability and validity of the data
- the validity of the conclusions.

The **reliability** of an investigation can be increased by…

- looking at relevant data from secondary sources (i.e. sources created by someone who did not experience first hand or participate in the original experiment)
- using an alternative method to check results
- ensuring results can be reproduced by others.

Science and Society

Scientific understanding can lead to technological developments. These developments can be exploited by different groups of people for different reasons. For example, the successful development of a new drug…

- benefits the drugs company financially
- improves the quality of life for patients
- can benefit society (e.g. if a new drug works, then maybe fewer people will be in hospital, which reduces time off sick, cost to the NHS, etc).

Scientific developments can raise certain **issues**. An issue is an important question that is in dispute and needs to be settled. The resolution of an issue may not be based on scientific evidence alone.

There are several different types of **issue** that can arise:

- **Social** – the impact on the human population of a community, city, country, or the world.
- **Economic** – money and related factors like employment and the distribution of resources.
- **Environmental** – the impact on the planet, its natural ecosystems and resources.
- **Ethical** – what is morally right or wrong; requires a value judgement to be made.

N.B. There is often an overlap between social and economic issues.

Peer Review

Finally, peer review is a process of self-regulation involving qualified professional individuals or experts in a particular field who examine the work undertaken critically. The vast majority of peer review methods are designed to maintain standards and provide credibility for the work that has been undertaken. These methods vary depending on the nature of the work and also on the overall purpose behind the review process.

Evaluating Information

It is important to be able to evaluate information relating to social-scientific issues, for both your GCSE course and to help you make informed decisions in life.

When evaluating information…
- make a list of **pluses** (pros)
- make a list of **minuses** (cons)
- consider how each point might **impact on society**.

You also need to consider whether the source of information is reliable and credible. Some important factors to consider are…
- **opinions**
- **bias**
- **weight of evidence**.

Opinions are personal viewpoints. Opinions backed up by valid and reliable evidence carry far more weight than those based on non-scientific ideas.

Opinions of experts can also carry more weight than non-experts.

Information is **biased** if it favours one particular viewpoint without providing a balanced account.

Biased information might include incomplete evidence or try to influence how you interpret the evidence.

Scientific evidence can be given **undue weight** or dismissed too quickly due to…
- political significance (consequences of the evidence could provoke public or political unrest)
- status of the experiment (e.g. if they do not have academic or professional status, experience, authority or reputation).

Limitations of Science

Although science can help us in lots of ways, it can't supply all the answers. We are still finding out about things and developing our scientific knowledge.

There are some questions that science can't answer. These tend to be questions…
- where beliefs, opinions and ethics are important
- where we don't have enough reproducible, repeatable or valid evidence.

Science can often tell us if something **can** be done, and **how** it can be done, but it can't tell us whether it **should** be done.

Decisions are made by individuals and by society on issues relating to science and technology.

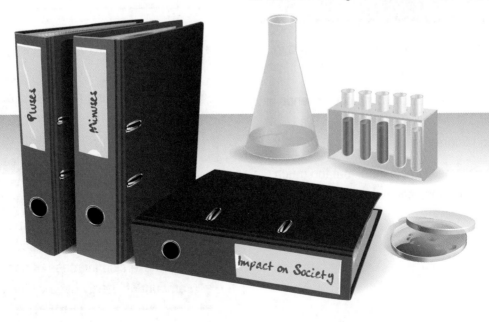

B1 Keeping Healthy

Diet and Exercise

A **healthy diet** contains the right balance of the different foods your body needs and provides the right amount of energy. **Carbohydrates**, **fats** and **proteins** are used by the body to release energy and to build cells. **Mineral ions** and **vitamins** are needed in small amounts for the body to function correctly.

A person is **malnourished** if their diet isn't balanced. A poor diet can lead to...

- a person being **overweight** or **obese**
- a person being **underweight**
- **deficiency diseases** or conditions such as **Type 2 diabetes**.

A person will lose weight (body mass) when the **amount of energy** in the food they eat is **less** than the amount of energy being used by their body.

Exercise **increases** the amount of energy used by the body.

A person's health is also affected by inherited factors including...

- **metabolic rate**
- **cholesterol level**.

Metabolic Rate

Metabolic rate is the rate at which all the **chemical reactions** in your body's cells are carried out. The rate is affected by...

- the amount of **activity or exercise** you do
- the **proportion of fat to muscle** in your body
- **inherited** factors.

Someone who exercises regularly is likely to be fitter and healthier than someone who doesn't exercise. The metabolic rate will stay high for some time after

finishing exercise. The less exercise that is taken and the warmer it is, the less food is needed.

Cholesterol

Cholesterol is made in your **liver** and is found in your **blood**. It is also found in some foods.

The amount of cholesterol in your blood depends on...

- your diet
- inherited factors.

Your body's cells need cholesterol, but too much cholesterol in the blood can increase the risk of **heart disease**.

Quick Test

1. Put the following people in order of how much energy they are likely to need in their diet (from highest to lowest): **a)** office worker **b)** professional athlete **c)** PE teacher.
2. What is the name given to the rate at which chemical reactions occur in the body?
3. What term is used to describe someone who does not eat a balanced diet?
4. Does exercise increase or decrease the amount of energy used by the body?

Key Words   Malnourished • Obesity • Deficiency disease • Metabolic rate • Cholesterol

Defence Against Infectious Diseases

Microorganisms that cause **infectious** diseases are called **pathogens**. The two main types of pathogens are...

* **bacteria**
* **viruses**.

The body has different ways of protecting itself against disease.

White blood cells help to defend against pathogens by...

* ingesting pathogens
* producing **antitoxins** to neutralise **toxins** from pathogens
* producing **antibodies** to destroy particular pathogens.

Bacteria...

* are very small
* reproduce rapidly
* may produce toxins that make you feel ill
* cause illnesses like tuberculosis (TB), tetanus and cholera.

Viruses...

* are smaller than bacteria
* reproduce rapidly once inside living cells, damaging the cells
* may produce toxins that make you feel ill
* cause illnesses like colds, flu, measles and polio.

Immunity and Vaccinations

When white blood cells produce specific **antibodies** to kill a pathogen it leads to **immunity** from that pathogen. This means that the white blood cells are sensitised to that particular pathogen and can produce the antibodies very quickly if it infects the body again.

You can **acquire** immunity to a particular disease by being **vaccinated** (immunised):

1 Small amounts of an **inactive or dead** pathogen are injected into your body.
2 Your white blood cells produce antibodies to destroy the pathogen.
3 You then have an **acquired immunity** to this particular pathogen because your white blood cells are sensitised to it, in the same way as if you had previously had the disease.

An example of a **vaccine** is the MMR vaccine used to protect children against measles, mumps and rubella.

If a large proportion of the population is immune to a pathogen, the pathogen spreads far less easily.

Preventing Disease

Semmelweiss was a doctor who worked in hospitals in the 1840s. He recognised how important good hygiene was in order to **prevent** infectious diseases spreading from one patient to another.

He insisted that doctors **wash their hands** before examining their patients. This greatly **reduced** the **number of deaths** from infectious diseases in his hospital.

Treatment of Disease

Some medicines, such as **painkillers** (e.g. aspirin), **relieve the symptoms** of infectious diseases, like headaches and fever. But these medicines don't kill pathogens.

Antibiotics (e.g. penicillin) **kill infective bacterial pathogens** inside the body. Antibiotics have greatly **reduced** the number of deaths from infectious bacterial diseases.

Antibiotics **don't kill viral pathogens**, which live and reproduce inside cells. It's difficult to develop drugs that kill viruses without damaging the body's own tissues.

Outbreaks of Disease

An **epidemic** is a local outbreak of a disease. A **pandemic** is a global outbreak of a disease and affects many more people than an epidemic, for example Swine Flu.

Mutations in bacteria and viruses, global travel and antibiotic resistance contribute to epidemics and pandemics.

Pandemics generally cause more deaths than epidemics as well as disrupting society and the economy.

Antibiotic Resistance

It's important that specific bacteria are treated with specific antibiotics.

Many **strains** of bacteria, including **MRSA** (Methicillin-resistant *Staphylococcus aureus*), have developed **resistance** to antibiotics as a result of **natural selection**.

Antibiotic-resistant strains occur when pathogens **mutate**:

1. A pathogen **mutates**, producing a new strain.
2. The new strain may be resistant to antibiotics.
3. The new resistant strain **spreads rapidly** because we are not immune to it and there is **no effective treatment**.

This means that new antibiotics need to be developed all the time.

The following factors contribute to an increase in the number of antibiotic-resistant strains of bacteria:
- **Overuse** of antibiotics.
- Prescribing **inappropriate antibiotics**.

So, it's important to **prevent** overuse of antibiotics.

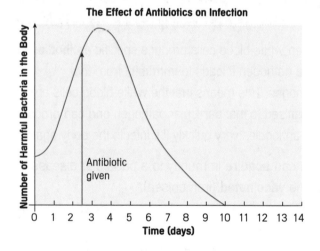

The Effect of Antibiotics on Infection

Number of Harmful Bacteria in the Body

Antibiotic given

Time (days)
0 1 2 3 4 5 6 7 8 9 10 11 12 13 14

(HT) When a bacterial infection is treated with antibiotics…
- the drugs kill individual pathogens of the non-resistant strain
- individual resistant pathogens **survive and reproduce**, so the population of resistant pathogens **rises**.

Nowadays, antibiotics are **not used** to treat non-serious infections, such as mild throat infections, in order to **slow down** the rate at which antibiotic-resistant strains develop.

Antibiotic • MRSA • Mutation

Investigating Microorganisms

You can **investigate** the effect of disinfectants and antibiotics on microorganisms in the laboratory using an **uncontaminated culture** of microorganisms.

Agar is most commonly used as the growth medium for microorganisms. It is a soft, jelly-like substance (made from seaweed) that melts easily and re-solidifies at around 50°C.

Nutrients are added to the agar to provide ideal growing conditions for microorganisms.

Preparing Uncontaminated Cultures

Uncontaminated cultures of microorganisms are prepared using the following procedures:

1 **Sterilisation of petri dishes and culture medium**
- Sterilise the **petri dishes** and **culture medium** in an **autoclave**.
- The high pressures and temperatures in the autoclave **kill** off **unwanted** microorganisms.

2 **Sterilisation of inoculating loops**
- Take an inoculating loop (made from nichrome wire with a wooden handle) and pick it up like a pen.
- Heat the loop and half the wire to red hot in a Bunsen flame, then leave to cool for five seconds.
- The loop is now **sterile** and can be used to transfer the microorganisms.
- Don't blow on the loop or wave it around to cool it as it will pick up unwanted microorganisms.

3 **Transferring microorganisms**
- Insert the inoculating loop into the container holding the microorganisms and transfer to the petri dish by wiping the loop on the surface of the agar.

4 **Sealing the petri dish**
- Close the petri dish and secure with tape to prevent microorganisms from the air contaminating the culture.
- Clearly label the dish on the base.
- Store upside down so **condensation** forms in the lid, not on the agar.

In schools and colleges, cultures are **incubated** at a maximum of 25°C to prevent the growth of potentially harmful **pathogens** that grow at body temperature (37°C).

In industry, higher temperatures can be used for more rapid growth.

Quick Test

1. What type of pathogen reproduces inside living cells?
2. What are headaches and fever examples of?
3. Who was responsible for insisting doctors wash their hands in hospitals?
4. What do white blood cells produce to kill pathogens?
5. How are bacterial pathogens that aren't affected by antibiotics described?

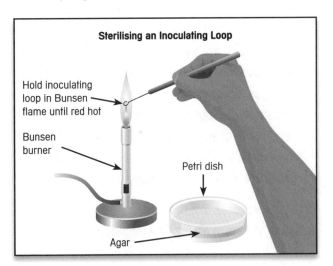

Sterilising an Inoculating Loop

Hold inoculating loop in Bunsen flame until red hot

Bunsen burner

Petri dish

Agar

B1 Nerves and Hormones

The Nervous System

Your nervous system allows you to...
- **react** to your surroundings
- **coordinate** your behaviour.

It consists of the following:
- The **brain** ⎱ The Central Nervous System
- The **spinal cord** ⎰ (CNS)
- **Nerves** (neurones)
- **Receptors**

Information from **receptors** in your sense organs passes along **neurones** (nerve cells) to your brain or spinal cord (CNS). The CNS then coordinates your response by sending instructions to **effectors**.

Effectors are either **muscles** or **glands**:
- Muscles respond by **contracting**.
- Glands respond by secreting (releasing) **chemical substances**, e.g. hormones.

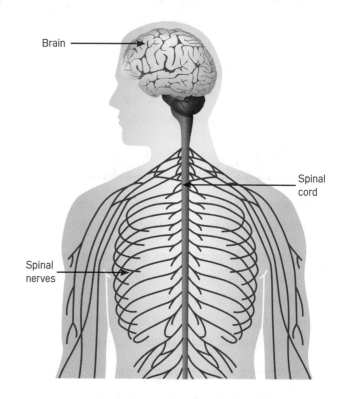

Brain

Spinal cord

Spinal nerves

Nervous System

| Receptor | Sensory Neurone | Relay Neurone | Brain and / or Spinal Cord | Motor Neurone | Effector |

Types of Receptor

Cells called **receptors** in your sense organs detect **stimuli** (changes in your environment). Different stimuli are detected by different receptors:
- Receptors in your **eyes** are sensitive to **light**.
- Receptors in your **ears** are sensitive to **sound** and **changes in position**, which help your balance.
- Receptors in your **nose** and on your **tongue** are sensitive to chemicals, helping you **smell** and **taste**.
- Receptors in your **skin** are sensitive to **touch**, **pressure**, **pain** and **temperature** changes.

Light receptor cells, like most animal cells, have a nucleus, cytoplasm and cell membrane.

The information about changes in your environment follows a pathway through your body to produce a response.

Nerve Pathway

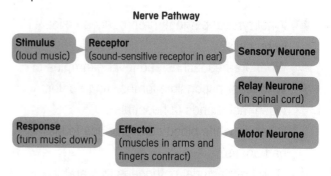

Stimulus (loud music) → Receptor (sound-sensitive receptor in ear) → Sensory Neurone → Relay Neurone (in spinal cord) → Motor Neurone → Effector (muscles in arms and fingers contract) → Response (turn music down)

This is all coordinated by your central nervous system, which receives information via sensory neurones.

Types of Neurone

Neurones are **specially adapted cells** that carry **electrical signals**, i.e. nerve impulses. There are three types of neurone, each with a slightly different function:

- **Sensory neurones** carry impulses from receptors to the CNS.
- **Motor neurones** carry signals from the CNS to effectors.
- **Relay neurones** carry impulses from one part of the CNS to another.

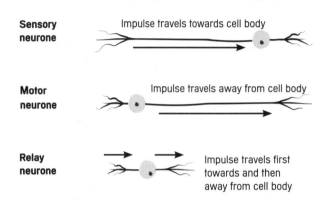

Connections Between Neurones

Neurones don't touch each other. There is a tiny gap between them called a **synapse**.

1. An electrical impulse travels through neurone A and reaches the synapse.
2. It is converted into chemicals, which diffuse across the gap.
3. Receptors on neurone B detect the chemicals.
4. An electrical impulse is generated in neurone B.

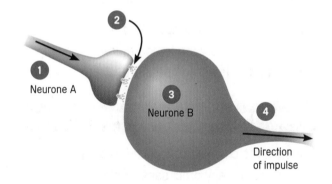

Reflex Actions

Reflex actions are designed to prevent your body from being harmed. For example, if you touch something hot, your hand automatically jerks away from it. If this was a conscious action, i.e. you had to think about the best way to respond, the process would be much slower and your hand would get burned.

Reflex actions are **automatic** and **quick**. They speed up your response time because they by-pass your brain. They involve sensory, relay and motor neurones. Your spinal cord acts as the **co-ordinator**.

1. Your **receptor** cells detect a stimulus.
2. An impulse travels along a **sensory** neurone.
3. The impulse is passed along a **relay** neurone in the spinal cord in the **CNS**.
4. The impulse travels along a **motor** neurone.
5. The impulse reaches the organ (**effector**) that brings about a response.

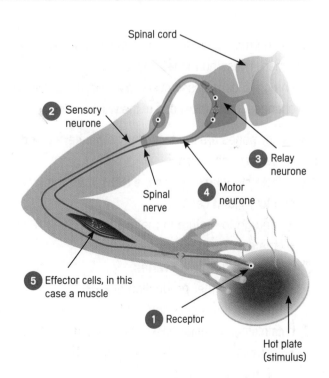

B1 Nerves and Hormones

Control in the Human Body

Humans need to keep their internal environment relatively constant. This means your body must control...

- **temperature** – to maintain the temperature at which enzymes work best (37°C)
- **water content** – 70% of body mass is water, which is vital for chemical reactions to take place properly
- **ion content** – if we don't have the correct balance of ions, our cells can become shrivelled, swollen or even burst
- **blood sugar** (glucose) levels – to provide your cells with a constant supply of energy.

Your body controls its **temperature** by...
- **shivering** to **increase** temperature
- **sweating** to **lower** temperature.

Water leaves the body in three ways:
- From the **lungs** when you **breathe out**.
- From the **skin** when your body **sweats** to cool down.
- Via the **kidneys** in **urine** (excess water only).

Ions are carried in water. Ions are lost...
- from the **skin** when your body **sweats**
- via the **kidneys** in **urine** (excess ions only).

Glucose is used up when it's converted to **energy**, e.g. for movement and to keep the body warm. You gain glucose, water and ions by eating and drinking.

Hormones and the Menstrual Cycle

Hormones are chemicals produced by **glands**. They...
- coordinate many processes within your body
- regulate the functions of many organs and cells
- usually travel to their **target** organs in the bloodstream.

Several hormones are involved in the **menstrual cycle** of women. These hormones cause...
- an egg to be released every month from the **ovaries**
- changes in the thickness of the **womb** lining.

These hormones are produced by the **pituitary gland** in the brain and the ovaries.

1 **Follicle stimulating hormone (FSH)** from the **pituitary gland** causes...
- an egg to mature in the ovaries
- the ovaries to produce oestrogen.

2 **Oestrogen** from the **ovaries**...
- inhibits further production of FSH
- causes the production of LH.

3 **Luteinising hormone (LH)** from the **pituitary gland**...
- stimulates the release of an egg in the middle of the menstrual cycle.

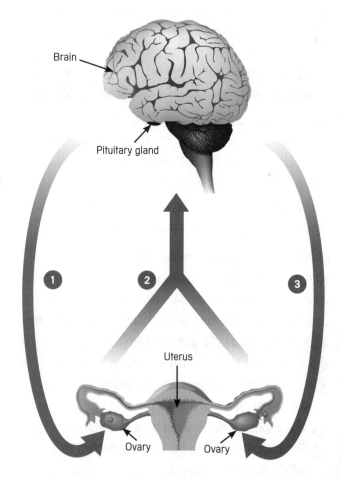

Brain

Pituitary gland

1   2   3

Uterus

Ovary   Ovary

Key Words   Hormone • Menstrual cycle • Pituitary gland • FSH • Oestrogen • LH

Artificial Control of Fertility

Hormones can be given to women to…

- **increase fertility** – women who don't produce enough FSH naturally can be given FSH and LH in a 'fertility drug' to simulate eggs to mature

- **reduce fertility** – oestrogen and progesterone can be given in **birth-control pills (oral contraceptives)** to prevent FSH production so that eggs don't mature.

The first birth-control pills contained large amounts of **oestrogen**, which made women suffer **side effects**.

Pills that only contain **progesterone** tend to have fewer side effects. Birth-control pills now contain much lower doses of oestrogen or are progesterone only.

Using fertility drugs increases the chance of multiple births, which increases the risk of complications during pregnancy.

In Vitro Fertilisation (IVF)

In vitro fertilisation (IVF) treatment is given to women who have difficulty becoming pregnant.

The main stages of IVF are as follows:

1. The mother is **given FSH** and **LH** to make several eggs mature.
2. The **eggs** are **collected** from the mother.
3. The eggs are **fertilised in a laboratory** using the father's sperm.
4. The fertilised eggs **develop into embryos** (tiny balls of cells).
5. One or two embryos are **inserted into** the mother's **uterus** (womb) to develop.

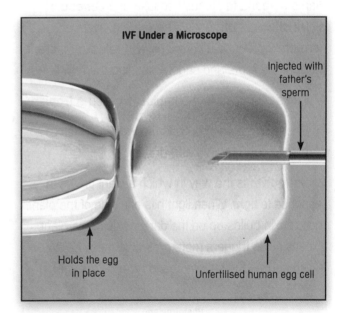

IVF Under a Microscope

Injected with father's sperm

Holds the egg in place

Unfertilised human egg cell

Quick Test

1. What is the gap between two neurones called?
2. When your eyes are exposed to a bright light your pupils automatically contract to protect the retina. What type of response is this?
3. There are three types of neurone.
   a) Which is responsible for sending impulses from the receptors to the central nervous system?
   b) Where do motor neurones carry electrical impulses to?
4. Why is it important to keep your body temperature constant at 37°C?
5. Where are FSH and LH produced in the body?
6. Which hormone causes the release of an egg from the ovaries?

Control in Plants

Plants as well as animals respond to **stimuli** (changes in their environment). Plants are sensitive to...

- **light** – their **shoots** grow **towards** the light
- **moisture** – their **roots** grow **towards** moisture
- **gravity** – **roots** grow in the **same direction** as the force of gravity (downwards); **shoots** grow **against** the force of **gravity** (upwards).

Plants produce hormones, called **plant growth substances**, that coordinate and control...

- the growth of shoots and roots
- the flowering of plants
- the ripening of fruit.

Plants respond to stimuli because of an **unequal distribution** of hormones. The varying levels of hormones produce different growth rates in different parts of the roots and shoots, causing them to bend.

A plant's response to a stimulus is called a **tropism**.

The hormone **auxin** controls the way in which plants respond to light and gravity.

Phototropism is the way in which a plant grows in response to **light**. When light hits one side of the plant, more auxin builds up on the darker side of the plant. Excess auxin triggers more growth in these cells, which causes the shoot to bend towards the light.

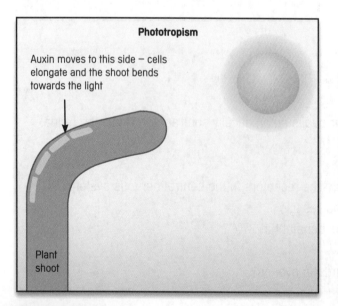

Phototropism

Auxin moves to this side – cells elongate and the shoot bends towards the light

Plant shoot

Gravitropism (or geotropism) is the way in which a plant grows in response to **gravity**.

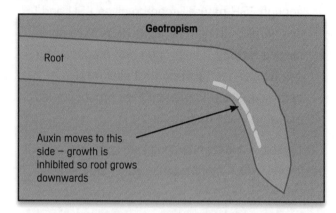

Geotropism

Root

Auxin moves to this side – growth is inhibited so root grows downwards

Plant growth hormones are used in agriculture and horticulture as...

- **weedkillers** – to selectively kill weeds by affecting the way in which they grow
- **rooting powders** – to stimulate roots to grow more quickly on plant cuttings.

WEED AWAY

Kills weeds, not grass

Quick Test

1. What are the three main external factors that affect plant growth?
2. What is the name of the hormone in plants that regulates growth?
3. What is a plant's response to light called?
4. Geotropism is a term used to describe a plant's response to what?
5. Why would a gardener use plant growth hormones?

Drugs

Drugs are chemical substances that alter the way the body works. They can be beneficial, but they can also harm the body.

- Some drugs can be obtained from **natural** substances (many have been known to indigenous peoples for years).
- Some drugs are **synthetic** (developed by scientists).

All drugs have an impact on your health because they interfere with chemical reactions taking place in your body. Medicinal drugs are designed to relieve disease and illness. Beneficial drugs like painkillers, antibiotics and statins are sometimes prescribed by doctor. Some painkillers can be bought in a pharmacy.

Statins are drugs used to lower the amount of cholesterol found in the blood. This then helps to reduce the risk of heart and circulatory disease. Prescribed statins are synthetic, although some statins occur naturally in certain foods.

Developing New Drugs

Scientists are continually developing new drugs.

When a new **medical drug** is devised, it has to be thoroughly **tested** and **trialled** before being used.

Drugs are tested in a series of stages to find out...

- if they are **toxic**
- if they are **efficient**
- what **dose** is needed.

The flow chart shows the main stages in developing a new drug.

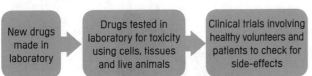

Using live tissues and animals as models allows scientists to predict how a drug may behave in humans. But some people disagree with this practice because they think it's unethical.

At the start of clinical trials, very low doses of the drug are used. If the drug is found to be safe, then more clinical trials take place using different doses to find out the **optimum** (most effective) dose for the drug.

In **double blind** trials, some patients are given a **placebo**, which does not contain the drug. Neither the doctor nor the patient knows who has received a placebo and who has received the drug until the trial is complete. This helps to reduce **bias** in the trial.

Thalidomide

The **thalidomide** drug was developed, tested and **approved** as a sleeping pill.

It was also found to be effective in relieving morning sickness in pregnant women, but it **hadn't been tested** for this use.

Thalidomide was **banned** when many pregnant women who took the drug gave birth to babies with severe limb abnormalities. Thalidomide was re-tested. It is now used to treat **leprosy**.

The thalidomide case has resulted in drug-testing becoming much more rigorous.

B1 The Use and Abuse of Drugs

Legal and Illegal Drugs

Some people use drugs for **recreation** (leisure), but if misused they can be harmful to the body.

- **Legal drugs**, e.g. alcohol and tobacco.
- **Illegal drugs**, e.g. heroin and cocaine, which are very addictive.

Drugs alter chemical processes in the body, so people can become dependent on, or **addicted** to, the drug.

Illegal recreational drugs, such as ecstasy, cannabis and heroin, may have adverse effects on the heart and circulatory system.

Once they are addicted, people will suffer **withdrawal symptoms** if they don't take the drug. Withdrawal symptoms may be **psychological** (e.g. paranoia) and /or **physical** (e.g. sweating and vomiting).

Some people believe taking recreational drugs will lead to hard drugs.

Types of Drug

Alcoholic drinks contain **ethanol**, which…

- affects the nervous system, causing reactions to slow down
- helps people to relax
- can lead to a lack of self control, unconsciousness, coma or death when taken in excess
- can lead to liver damage or brain damage in the long term.

Tobacco smoke contains **carbon monoxide**, nicotine (which is addictive) and **carcinogens**.

Smoking tobacco can cause…

- emphysema – damage to the alveoli caused by coughing
- bronchitis
- heart disease
- lung cancer.

The carbon monoxide in tobacco smoke reduces the oxygen-carrying capacity of the blood. In pregnant women this can deprive the **fetus** of oxygen, leading to a **low birth mass**.

Cannabis is an illegal drug. Cannabis smoke contains chemicals that may cause mental illness in some people.

There are several types of drug that an athlete can use to enhance their performance.

Some of these drugs are banned by law and some are legally available on prescription, but all are prohibited by sporting regulations. This is because they give athletes an unfair advantage and are dangerous when taken without medical advice.

Examples include…

- stimulants that boost bodily functions such as heart rate
- anabolic steroids that simulate muscle growth.

Quick Test

1. What do we call a chemical substance that alters the way in which the body works?
2. What is the name given to 'dummy' drugs used in medical trials?
3. How does alcohol affect a person's reactions?
4. What is the name of the addictive substance found in cigarettes?
5. Why are steroids banned in sport?

Competition

In order to **survive** and **reproduce**, organisms need materials from their environment and from the other organisms that live there. Organisms **compete** with each other for these materials.

Plants compete with each other for...

- light
- space
- water
- nutrients from the soil.

When organisms (including microorganisms) compete, those that are **better adapted** to their environment are more successful. As a result, the population grows. This often leads to the exclusion of other competing organisms.

Animals compete with each other for...

- food
- mates
- territory.

Adaptations

Adaptations are features that make an organism well-suited to its environment. Adaptations increase an organism's chance of **survival**. Animals and plants may be adapted for survival in the conditions where they normally live, e.g. deserts and the Arctic.

Adaptations to the following features can help animals survive in arctic or dry environments:

- Changes to surface area.
- Thickness of insulating coat.
- Amount of body fat.
- Camouflage.

Plants may be adapted to survive in dry environments by...

- changes to surface area, particularly leaves that are often reduced in size
- water-storage tissues
- extensive root systems.

Extremophiles are organisms that live in environments that are very extreme. Extremophiles can be tolerant to high salt levels, temperatures or pressures.

Animals and plants may be adapted to cope with specific features of their environment. For example...

- some plants (e.g. cacti and roses) have thorns to prevent animals eating them
- some animals (e.g. blue dart frogs) have developed poisons and warning colours to keep **predators** away.

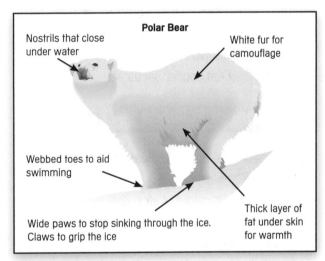

Polar Bear

Nostrils that close under water

White fur for camouflage

Webbed toes to aid swimming

Wide paws to stop sinking through the ice. Claws to grip the ice

Thick layer of fat under skin for warmth

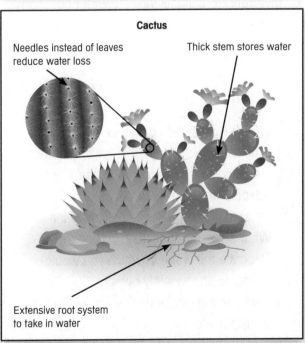

Cactus

Needles instead of leaves reduce water loss

Thick stem stores water

Extensive root system to take in water

B1 Interdependence and Adaptation

Environmental Change

The distribution of animals and plants can be affected by changes in the **environment**. Changes can be due to…

- **living factors** – such as a change in a competitor
- **non-living factors** – such as a change in the average temperature or rainfall.

Examples

Red and **grey squirrels** live in the same habitat and eat the same food. But the native red squirrel is unable to compete with the very well adapted grey squirrel, which was introduced to the UK in the 19th century. The grey squirrel has outcompeted the red squirrel in deciduous woodlands, which has forced the red squirrel to live in coniferous woodlands where they can eat conifer seeds.

Indicators of Pollution

Living organisms can be **indicators of pollution**. For example…

- **lichens** are indicators of **air** pollution, as their growth is affected by sulfur dioxide concentrations in the atmosphere
- **invertebrate** animals indicate **water** pollution and are used as indicators of the concentration of dissolved oxygen in water.

Bees are very important in our ecosystems because they pollinate many plants including wild flowers and food crops. Einstein said that if there were no more bees on our planet, mankind would die out within four years! The distribution of bees has changed in recent years, with America and Germany reporting the highest bee loss. Experts say that disease, habitat loss or climate change has caused the change in bee distribution.

Measuring Environmental Change

Environmental changes such as oxygen levels, temperature and rainfall can be measured using specialist **equipment**. Data loggers are often used by scientists to measure environmental factors because they are reasonably accurate.

Examples

Stonefly nymph are found in clean water with high levels of dissolved oxygen.

The **rat-tailed maggot** will tolerate low levels of oxygen and is found in polluted water.

Stonefly Nymph

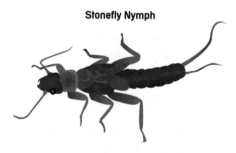

Rat-tailed Maggot

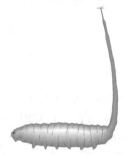

Quick Test

1. What resources do plants compete for?
2. Why have cacti adapted to have thorns?
3. List four ways in which polar bears are adapted to live in the Arctic.
4. What might the absence of lichens indicate?
5. What are extremophiles?
6. Describe the water in which you would expect to find stonefly nymph.
7. Give one reason for the decline of the distribution of bees.

Food Chains

Radiation from the Sun is the source of **energy** for all **communities** of living organisms.

Green plants and algae capture a **small fraction** of the solar energy that reaches them. They use **photosynthesis** to transfer light energy into **chemical** energy. This energy is **stored** in the cells of the plant.

When other organisms eat the plant, they gain the stored energy. This transfer of energy can be represented by a **food chain**.

Food Chain

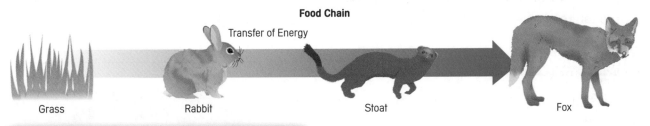

Transfer of Energy

Grass   Rabbit   Stoat   Fox

Pyramids of Biomass

The **biomass** (mass of living material) at each stage in a food chain is less than it was at the previous stage.

This can be drawn to scale and shown as a **pyramid of biomass**.

Biomass and energy are lost at every stage of a food chain due to several factors:
- Materials and energy are **lost** in the organism's **waste materials**.
- Much of the energy released through **respiration** (for **heat** and **movement**) is eventually transferred to the surroundings.

Efficient food **production** involves conserving as much energy as possible.

This can be achieved by...
- reducing the number of stages in a food chain
- limiting an animal's movement
- controlling an animal's temperature.

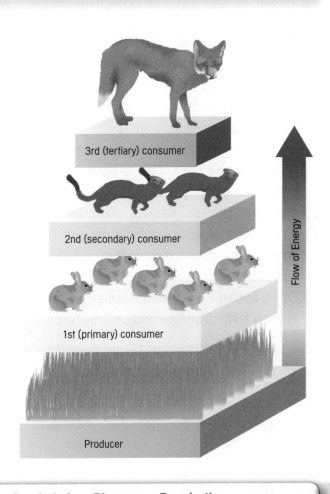

3rd (tertiary) consumer

2nd (secondary) consumer

1st (primary) consumer

Producer

Flow of Energy

B1 Waste Materials from Plants and Animals

Decay Processes

Living organisms remove materials from the environment for growth and other processes. When the organisms excrete waste or die and decay, the materials are **returned** to the environment.

Microorganisms (e.g. bacteria and fungi) break down (digest) waste and dead bodies. This **decay** process releases substances needed by plants for growth.

Microorganisms digest materials faster in conditions that are **warm**, **moist** and **aerobic** (rich in oxygen).

In a stable community, two processes are balanced:
- The **removal** of materials from the environment.
- The **return** of materials to the environment.

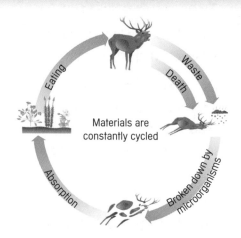

Materials are constantly cycled

In order to reduce household waste, organic kitchen matter and garden waste can be recycled in compost heaps or through council collection schemes.

The Carbon Cycle

The constant cycling of carbon is called the **carbon cycle**.

1. Carbon dioxide (CO_2) is **removed** from the environment by green plants and algae for **photosynthesis**. Some CO_2 is returned to the atmosphere when green plants and algae respire.
2. Plants and algae use carbon from CO_2 to make carbohydrates, fats and proteins. When plants and algae are eaten by animals (and these animals are eaten by other animals), some of the carbon becomes part of the fats and proteins that make up their bodies.
3. Animals respire, releasing CO_2 into the atmosphere.
4. When plants, algae and animals die, some animals and microorganisms feed on their bodies causing them to break down.
5. CO_2 is released into the atmosphere when **detritus** feeders and microorganisms respire.

When wood and fossil fuels are burned (combustion) carbon dioxide is released into the atmosphere.

By the time a cycle is completed, all the energy originally absorbed by the green plants has been transferred.

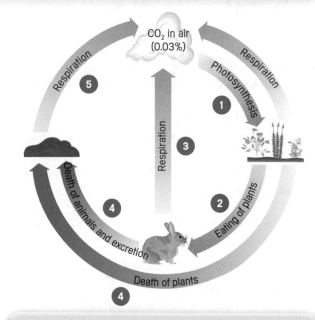

Quick Test

1. List three conditions required by microorganisms for decay.
2. Which process releases carbon dioxide into the atmosphere?
3. Give two ways in which energy is lost from a food chain.
4. What do we call the mass of living material in a population?

Key Words   Decay • Aerobic • Carbon cycle • Photosynthesis • Detritus

Genetic Information

The nucleus of a cell contains **chromosomes**.

- **Chromosomes** are made up of **DNA**.
- A section of chromosome is called a **gene**.
- Different **genes** control the development of different **characteristics**.

During **sexual reproduction**, genes are passed from parents to offspring in the **gametes** (sex cells). This is how certain characteristics are **inherited**.

Chromosomes come in **pairs**, but different species have different numbers of pairs, e.g. humans have **23 pairs**, dogs have 39 pairs.

A Section of One Chromosome

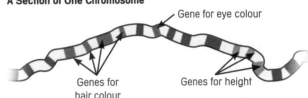

Variation

Differences between the characteristics of individuals of the same species are called **variation**. Variation may be due to…

- the genes they have inherited (**genetic factors**), e.g. the different colours of dog coats
- the conditions in which they have developed (**environmental factors**), e.g. identical twins may be very different in mass due to different eating habits
- a **combination** of genetic and environmental factors, e.g. weight.

Reproduction

There are two types of reproduction:

- **Sexual reproduction**.
- **Asexual reproduction**.

During **sexual reproduction** male and female **gametes** fuse together. This is called **fertilisation**. The genes carried by the egg and the sperm are mixed together to produce a new individual. This process produces lots of **variation**, even amongst offspring from the same parents.

Asexual reproduction doesn't produce any genetic variation at all. Only one parent is needed, so there is no mixing of genes. All offspring are genetically **identical** to the parent, i.e. **clones**. Variation can only be due to environmental factors.

B1 Genetic Variation and its Control

Reproducing Plants

Plants can reproduce **asexually** to produce **clones**. Many plants naturally reproduce asexually, e.g. spider plants, strawberry plants and potato plants.

Many plants can be reproduced asexually **by artificial means**. For example, you can take **cuttings** from a plant with desired characteristics to produce clones quickly and cheaply. These plants are genetically identical to the parent plant.

Cloning Techniques

These are some **modern** cloning techniques.

Tissue Culture

1 Small groups of cells are scraped from part of a plant.
2 The cells are grown on agar containing nutrients and hormones.

The offspring are **genetically identical to the parent plant**.

Embryo Transplants

1 Cells from a developing animal embryo are split **before** they become **specialised**.
2 The resulting identical embryos are transplanted into host mothers.

The offspring are **genetically identical to each other, but not to the parents**.

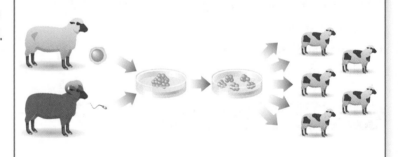

Adult Cell Cloning

1 The nucleus is removed from an **unfertilised egg cell**.
2 The nucleus from an adult body cell, e.g. skin cell, is then inserted into the 'empty' egg cell.
3 An electric shock causes the egg cell to begin dividing to form an embryo.
4 The embryo is inserted into a host mother.

The offspring is **genetically identical to the donor animal** (that the nucleus came from).

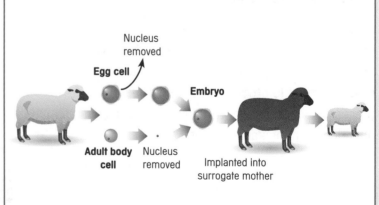

Nucleus removed

Egg cell

Embryo

Adult body cell

Nucleus removed

Implanted into surrogate mother

Genetic Modification

Genetic modification (**genetic engineering**) involves transferring genetic material from one organism to another:

1. Individual **genes** are '**cut out**' of the chromosomes of an organism using special **enzymes**
2. The genes are then transferred to the cells of other organisms.

Genes can be transferred to the cells of animals and plants at an early stage in their development so that they develop with **desired characteristics.**

In crop plants, desirable characteristics might include...

- improved yield (more food per plant)
- improved resistance to pests or herbicides
- a longer shelf life.

Crops that have had their genes modified are called **genetically modified crops** (**GM crops**).

Some people have concerns about GM crops. These concerns include...

- the effect of GM crops on populations of wild **flowers** and **insects**
- the uncertainty about the effects of eating GM crops on **human health**.

GM-FREE FOR ME!

Quick Test

1. What are chromosomes made from?
2. What is a section of chromosome called?
3. How many pairs of chromosomes are found in a human liver cell?
4. Which type of reproduction produces lots of variation in the offspring?
5. What term is used to describe the offspring of asexual reproduction?
6. In which cloning technique would you expect to find offspring that are genetically identical to each other, but not to the parents?
7. What is used to cut out genes from chromosomes?
8. Describe one concern about GM crops.

B1 Evolution

Studying Evolution

Studying the similarities and differences between organisms helps us to…

- **classify** living organisms into animals, plants and microorganisms
- understand evolutionary and ecological **relationships**.

Evidence of how organisms have changed over time comes from **fossils** found in rocks.

Evolutionary trees are models that allow us to map the relationships between organisms.

There are different theories of evolution because scientists don't always have enough valid or reliable evidence.

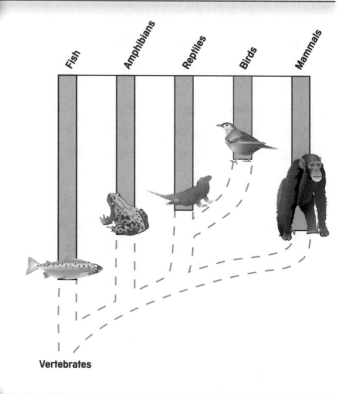

Fish   Amphibians   Reptiles   Birds   Mammals

Vertebrates

Theories of Evolution

Charles **Darwin's** theory of evolution by **natural selection** states: all living things that exist today, and many more that are now **extinct, evolved** from **simple life forms** that first developed more than three billion years ago.

Darwin's *The Theory of Evolution by Natural Selection* was published in 1859. It took a long time to be accepted because…

- it **challenged** the idea that God made all the animals and plants that live on Earth
- there was **insufficient evidence** at that time to convince many scientists
- the **mechanism of inheritance and variation** wasn't discovered until 50 years later.

Jean-Baptiste **Lamarck** described another theory of evolution: any **change** that occurs during the lifetime of an organism will be passed on and inherited by their offspring.

We now know that in the vast majority of cases this type of inheritance can't occur.

Lamarck believed that the necks of giraffes stretched during their lifetime to reach food in trees. They then passed this characteristic on to the next generation.

Darwin believed giraffes that had longer necks could reach more food in trees, so they were more likely to survive and reproduce (survival of the fittest).

Key Words   Fossil • Natural selection • Extinct • Evolve

Evolution by Natural Selection

Evolution...
- is the change in a population over **many generations**
- may result in the formation of a new species, which is **better adapted** to its environment.

1 Individual organisms within a species show **variation** because of differences in their genes.

2 Individuals better adapted to their environment are more likely to survive, breed successfully and produce offspring. This is **survival of the fittest**.

3 The survivors pass on their genes to their offspring, resulting in an 'improved' organism **evolving** through **natural selection**.

Gene **mutations** may bring about a more rapid change in a species.

Example

1 Peppered moths were pale in colour, so they were **camouflaged** against the bark of silver birch trees. Predators found it hard to see (and eat) them.

2 During the Industrial Revolution the air became polluted and silver birch trees turned black with soot.

3 Darker coloured moths were now better camouflaged on the trees. More survived and reproduced, and the population of darker moths grew.

Dark Peppered Moth

Peppered Moth

Quick Test

1 Who developed the theory of evolution by natural selection?

2 Give one reason why the theory of evolution by natural selection was not accepted straight away.

3 Who described a theory of evolution where changes during the lifetime of an organism were passed on to the next generation?

4 Where can evidence be found to support the theory of evolution?

5 What can cause more rapid changes in the genes of a species?

6 Why do individuals within a species show variation?

1 High blood cholesterol level is linked with coronary heart disease.

a) Where is cholesterol made in your body? .... **(1 mark)**

b) Name two factors that can affect the amount of cholesterol found in your blood.

....

.... **(2 marks)**

2 By the time a baby is six months old they have been routinely offered seven vaccinations by the NHS. The vaccination programme continues as a child gets older.

a) What is found in a vaccine?

.... **(1 mark)**

b) What do your white blood cells produce in response to a vaccine?

.... **(1 mark)**

c) Not all diseases can be vaccinated against, so doctors may need to prescribe antibiotics to help you fight them. What type of pathogen do antibiotics work against?

.... **(1 mark)**

3 A student wanted to investigate the effect of different cleaning products on the growth of bacteria. She set up five agar plates that were seeded with one type of bacteria. On each plate the student placed four discs that had been soaked in a particular cleaning product. The plates were incubated at 25°C for three days. The student then measured the diameter around the discs where the bacteria hadn't grown. Her results are shown in the table below.

Plate and Cleaning Product	Diameter (mm) Around Each Disc where Bacteria hasn't Grown				Mean (mm)
	Disc 1	Disc 2	Disc 3	Disc 4	
Plate 1 (soap)	1	2	2	1	1.5
Plate 2 (hand wash)	3	2	2	4	2.75
Plate 3 (kitchen cleaner)	5	4	6	5	5
Plate 4 (bathroom cleaner)	5	5	6	7	....
Plate 5 (no cleaner)	0	0	0	0	0

a) Complete the table by calculating the mean diameter where bacteria didn't grow for Plate 4. **(1 mark)**

b) Which was the most effective product at killing the bacteria?

.... **(1 mark)**

c) Why did the student use 'Plate 5 (no cleaner)'?

.... **(1 mark)**

d) How has the student made her results reliable?

.... **(1 mark)**

4 Reflex actions are designed to prevent your body from being harmed.

a) What type of neurone carries a signal to your spinal cord in a reflex action?

.... **(1 mark)**

b) A response is created by an impulse being sent along a motor neurone to reach which type of organ?

.... **(1 mark)**

c) What is the junction between two neurones called? .... **(1 mark)**

5 The female menstrual cycle is controlled by hormones that cause eggs to be released and cause changes to the thickness of the womb lining.

a) Which hormone is secreted from the pituitary gland and causes eggs to mature in the ovaries?

.... **(1 mark)**

b) Which hormone is released from the ovaries? .... **(1 mark)**

c) Explain how hormones can be given to women to...

i) increase fertility? ....

.... **(1 mark)**

ii) reduce fertility? ....

.... **(1 mark)**

6 **a)** The most common legal drug taken in this country is alcohol. Give one effect of alcohol on the body.

.... **(1 mark)**

b) Tobacco is another legalised drug in this country. Give one effect of tobacco on the body.

.... **(1 mark)**

7 Arctic foxes live in cold conditions. They have adapted to increase their chance of survival. List two adaptations of the arctic fox and explain why it helps the fox to survive.

a) ....

....

....

....

....

....

b) ....

....

C1 The Fundamental Ideas in Chemistry

Atoms and Elements

All substances are made of **atoms** (very small particles). Each atom has a small central **nucleus** made up of **protons** and **neutrons**. The nucleus is surrounded by orbiting **electrons**.

A substance that contains only one sort of atom is called an **element**. There are about 100 different elements.

The atoms of each element are represented by a different **chemical symbol**.

For example...
- sodium = Na
- carbon = C
- iron = Fe

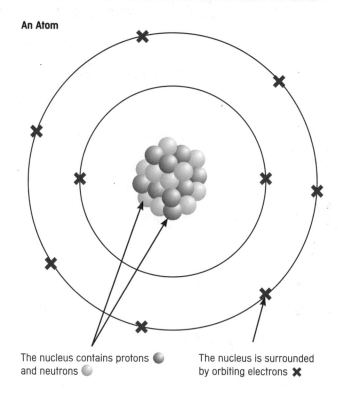

An Atom

The nucleus contains protons and neutrons

The nucleus is surrounded by orbiting electrons ✖

The Periodic Table

Elements are arranged in the **Periodic Table**. The **groups** in the Periodic Table contain elements that have similar properties.

For example, all Group 1 elements (the alkali metals) react vigorously with water to produce an alkaline solution and hydrogen gas.

The Group 1 elements react rapidly with oxygen to form metal oxides. The elements in Group 0 are called the noble gases. They are all unreactive elements because their atoms have full outer shells of electrons, meaning they are stable. Atoms of noble gases have eight electrons in their outer shell, except for helium, which only has two.

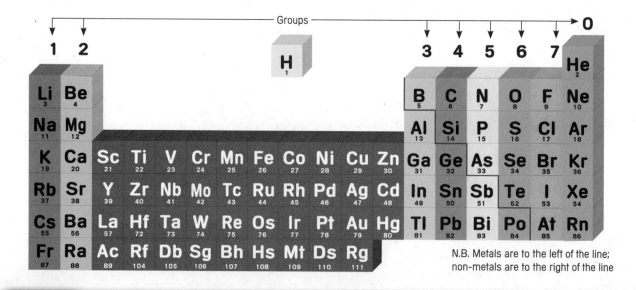

N.B. Metals are to the left of the line; non-metals are to the right of the line

Key Words   Atom • Nucleus • Proton • Neutron • Electron • Element

Atomic Structure

Protons, neutrons and electrons have relative **electrical charges**.

Atomic Particle	Relative Charge
Proton	+1
Neutron	0
Electron	-1

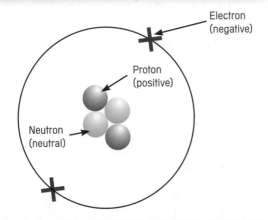

Atoms, as a whole, have **no overall charge** because they contain an **equal number** of **protons** and **electrons**.

All atoms of a particular element have the **same number of protons**. Atoms of different elements have **different numbers** of **protons**. The number of protons in an atom is called its **atomic number**. The sum of the protons and neutrons in an atom is its **mass number**.

Elements are arranged in the modern Periodic Table in order of **atomic number**.

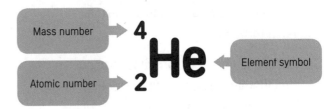

The number of neutrons in an atom is calculated by:

Mass number — **Atomic number**

Electron Configuration and Structure

Electrons in an atom occupy the lowest available **energy level** (i.e. the innermost available shell). For the first 20 elements:

- The **first** level can only contain a **maximum** of **two electrons**.
- The energy levels after this can each hold a **maximum** of **eight electrons**.

The **electron configuration** tells us how the electrons are arranged around the nucleus in **energy levels** or **shells**. It is written as a series of numbers, for example...

- oxygen is 2,6
- aluminium is 2,8,3

The **Periodic Table** groups the elements in terms of **electronic structure**.

Elements in the **same group** have the same number of **electrons** in their **highest energy level (outer shell)**

and this gives them **similar chemical properties**. A particular energy level is gradually filled with electrons from **left to right**, across each **period**.

Electronic configurations can also be represented as shown below.

Sodium 2,8,1

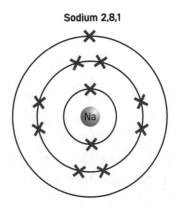

You need to be able to represent the electronic structure of the first 20 elements.

Compounds

When elements react their atoms join with other atoms to form **compounds**. This involves…

- the **giving** and **taking** of electrons to form ions **OR**
- the **sharing** of electrons to form **molecules**.

Metal atoms lose electrons to form positive ions and non-metal atoms gain electrons to form negative ions. Compounds formed between metals and non-metals consist of ions. Compounds formed between non-metal atoms form molecules. Atoms in molecules are held together by covalent bonds.

Chemical Formulae

Compounds are represented by a combination of numbers and chemical symbols called a **chemical formula**.

Scientists use **chemical formulae** to show…
- the different elements in a compound
- the number of atoms of each element in the compound.

In chemical formulae, the position of the numbers tells you what is multiplied:
- A small number that sits below the line multiplies only the symbol that comes immediately before it.
- A number that is the same size as the letters multiplies all the symbols that come after it.

For example…
- H_2O means $(2 \times H) + (1 \times O)$
- $2NaOH$ means $2 \times (NaOH)$ or $2 \times (Na + O + H)$.

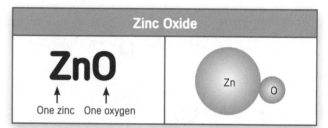

Zinc Oxide

ZnO

One zinc   One oxygen

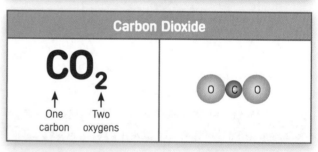

Carbon Dioxide

CO₂

One carbon   Two oxygens

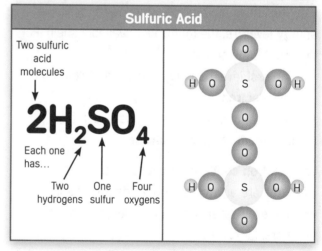

Sulfuric Acid

Two sulfuric acid molecules

2H₂SO₄

Each one has…
Two hydrogens   One sulfur   Four oxygens

Quick Test

1. Which two particles are found in the nucleus of an atom?
2. What is the connection between the number of electrons in the highest energy level of an atom (the outer shell) and the group the element is in?
3. What is the electron configuration of an atom of magnesium?

Chemical Reactions

You can show what has happened during a **chemical reaction** by writing a **word** or **symbol equation**.

The **reactants** (i.e. the substances that react) are on one side of the equation and the **products** (i.e. the new substances that are formed) are on the other.

The total mass of the products of a chemical reaction is always equal to the total mass of the reactants. This is because **no atoms are lost or made**. The products of a chemical reaction are made up from exactly the same atoms as the reactants.

Chemical symbol equations must always be **balanced**. There must be the same number of atoms of each element on the reactant side of the equation as there is on the product side.

Number of atoms of each element on reactants side	=	Number of atoms of each element on products side

Example

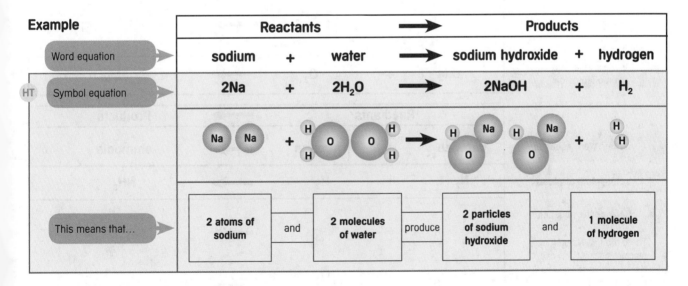

	Reactants	→	Products
Word equation	sodium + water	→	sodium hydroxide + hydrogen
Symbol equation (HT)	2Na + 2H₂O	→	2NaOH + H₂

Symbol equation: $2Na + 2H_2O \longrightarrow 2NaOH + H_2$

This means that...

2 atoms of sodium	and	2 molecules of water	produce	2 particles of sodium hydroxide	and	1 molecule of hydrogen

C1 The Fundamental Ideas in Chemistry

HT Writing Balanced Equations

The following steps tell you how to write a balanced equation.

1. Write a word equation for the chemical reaction.

2. Substitute formulae for the elements or compounds.

3. Balance the equation by adding numbers in front of the reactants and / or products.

4. Write down the balanced symbol equation.

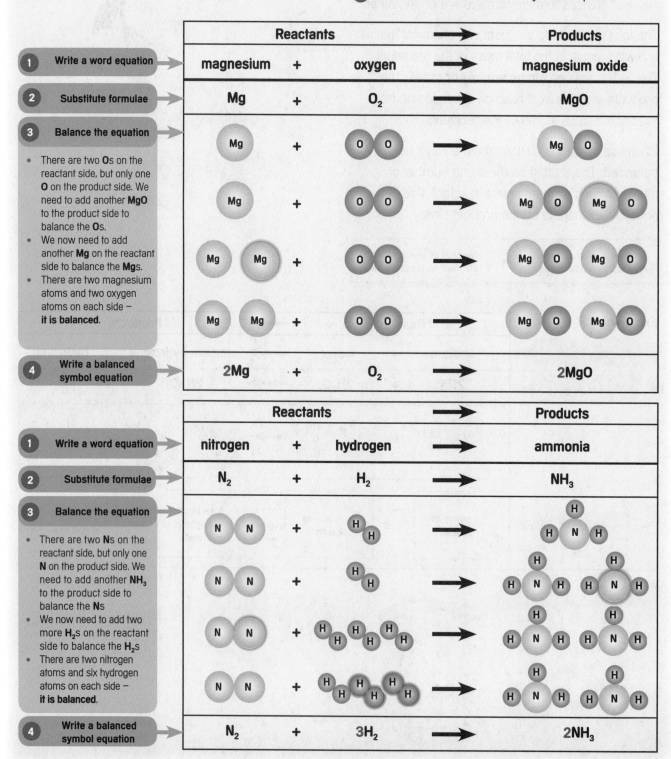

1. **Write a word equation** — magnesium + oxygen → magnesium oxide

2. **Substitute formulae** — Mg + O_2 → MgO

3. **Balance the equation**

- There are two **O**s on the reactant side, but only one **O** on the product side. We need to add another **MgO** to the product side to balance the **O**s.
- We now need to add another **Mg** on the reactant side to balance the **Mg**s.
- There are two magnesium atoms and two oxygen atoms on each side — **it is balanced**.

4. **Write a balanced symbol equation** — $2Mg$ + O_2 → $2MgO$

1. **Write a word equation** — nitrogen + hydrogen → ammonia

2. **Substitute formulae** — N_2 + H_2 → NH_3

3. **Balance the equation**

- There are two **N**s on the reactant side, but only one **N** on the product side. We need to add another **NH$_3$** to the product side to balance the **N**s
- We now need to add two more **H$_2$**s on the reactant side to balance the **H$_2$**s
- There are two nitrogen atoms and six hydrogen atoms on each side — **it is balanced**.

4. **Write a balanced symbol equation** — N_2 + $3H_2$ → $2NH_3$

Limestone (CaCO₃)

Limestone is a **sedimentary rock** consisting mainly of **calcium carbonate**. It is cheap, easy to obtain and has many uses.

Limestone can be used…
- as a building material
- for making cement, mortar and concrete.

As a building material

Limestone can be quarried, cut into blocks and used to build houses. It can be **eroded** by **acid rain** but this is a very slow process.

Heating limestone

When calcium carbonate is heated in a kiln it **decomposes**. This reaction is called **thermal decomposition**. It causes the calcium carbonate to break down into calcium oxide and carbon dioxide.

Magnesium, copper, zinc, calcium and sodium carbonates decompose on heating in a similar way.

Some metal carbonates, e.g. others in Group 1, may not decompose at the temperatures reached by a Bunsen burner.

The calcium oxide can then be reacted with water to produce calcium hydroxide. Calcium hydroxide can be used to neutralise soils and lakes, preventing crop failure.

Carbonates of other metals decompose in a similar way when they're heated.

Making cement, mortar and concrete

Powdered limestone is roasted in a rotary kiln with powdered clay to produce dry **cement**. When sand and water are mixed in, **mortar** is produced.

Mortar is used to hold bricks and stones together. When aggregate, sand and water are mixed in, **concrete** is produced.

Reacting Carbonates with Dilute Acid

Carbonates react with **dilute acids** to form **carbon dioxide** gas (and a salt and water). Carbon dioxide turns limewater (a solution of calcium hydroxide in water) cloudy. For example…

calcium carbonate	+	hydrochloric acid	→	calcium chloride	+	carbon dioxide	+	water

$$CaCO_3(s) + 2HCl(aq) \longrightarrow CaCl_2(aq) + CO_2(g) + H_2O(l)$$

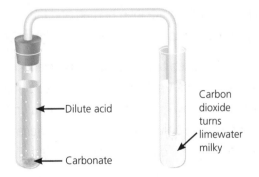

Carbon dioxide turns limewater milky

Dilute acid

Carbonate

Quick Test

1. Calcium carbonate can be decomposed upon heating (thermal decomposition) to make which two compounds?
2. What is the chemical test for carbon dioxide gas?
3. What substance is powdered limestone mixed with to make cement?
4. **HT** Balance the following equations:
   a) $Al + O_2 \longrightarrow Al_2O_3$
   b) $Cr + HCl \longrightarrow CrCl_3 + H_2$

C1 Metals and their Uses

Ores

The Earth's crust contains many naturally occurring **elements** and **compounds** called **minerals**.

A **metal ore** is a mineral that contains enough metal to make it economically viable to extract it. Over time it may become more or less economic to extract a metal from an ore as technology develops.

Ores are mined and impurities may be removed before the metal is extracted and purified.

This mining can involve the digging up and processing of large amounts of rock.

Extracting Metals from their Ores

The method of metal extraction depends on **how reactive the metal is**.

Unreactive metals, like gold, exist naturally in the earth and can be obtained through panning. But most metals are found as **metal oxides**, or as compounds that can be easily changed into a metal oxide.

Metals that are **less reactive than carbon** can be extracted from their oxides by heating with carbon, e.g. iron and lead.

Metals **more reactive than carbon**, e.g. aluminium, are extracted by electrolysis of molten compounds.

Extraction of Copper

Copper is a useful metal because it is a good conductor of electricity and heat. It is easily bent into shape yet hard enough to be used to make water pipes and tanks. It does not react with water so lasts for a long time.

Copper can be extracted from copper-rich ores by heating the ores in a furnace. This process is known as **smelting**. This copper can then be purified by **electrolysis**. Copper can also be obtained from solutions of copper salts by electrolysis or by displacement using scrap iron.

During electrolysis the positive copper ions move towards the negative electrode and form pure copper metal.

But the mining of more copper means that we are running out of copper-rich ores. So, new methods have been developed to extract copper from ores that contain less copper.

Copper can be extracted from:
- Low-grade ores (ores that contain small amounts of copper)
- Contaminated land by **phytomining** or by **bioleaching**. These two methods are more environmentally friendly than traditional mining methods.

Phytomining is a method that uses plants to absorb copper. As the plants grow they absorb (and store) copper. The plants are then burned and the ash produced contains copper in relatively high quantities.

Bioleaching uses bacteria to extract metals from low-grade ores. A solution containing bacteria is mixed with a low-grade ore. The bacteria convert the copper into solution (known as a leachate solution) where it can be easily extracted.

Mineral • Ore • Smelting • Electrolysis • Phytomining • Bioleaching

Iron

Iron oxide can be reduced in a blast furnace to produce **iron**. Molten iron obtained from a blast furnace contains roughly…

- 96% iron
- 4% carbon and other metals.

Because it is impure the iron is very brittle, with limited uses. To produce pure iron, all the **impurities** have to be removed.

The **atoms** in pure iron are arranged in layers that can slide over each other easily. This makes pure iron soft and malleable. It can be easily shaped, but it's too soft for many practical uses.

The properties of iron can be changed by mixing it with small quantities of carbon or other metals to make **steel**. The majority of iron is converted into steel. Steel is an **alloy**.

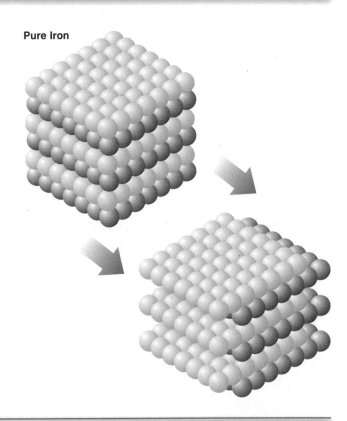

Pure Iron

Alloys

Many of the metals you come across every day are alloys. Pure copper, gold and aluminium are too soft for many uses, so they are mixed with small amounts of similar metals to make them harder for items in everyday use, for example coins.

Steel

Carbon is added to iron to make the alloy **steel**.

Alloys like steel are developed to have the necessary properties for a specific purpose.

In steel, the amount of carbon and / or other elements determines its properties:

- Steel with a high carbon content is hard and strong.
- Steel with a low carbon content is soft and easily shaped.
- **Stainless steel** is hard and resistant to corrosion.

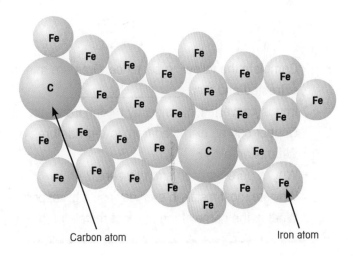

Carbon atom

Iron atom

C1 Metals and their Uses

The Transition Metals

Between Groups 2 and 3 in the Periodic Table is a block of metallic elements called the **transition metals**.

The transition metals...

- are good **conductors** of heat and electricity
- are hard and mechanically strong
- have high melting points (except mercury)
- can be bent or hammered into shape.

These properties make the transition metals very useful as structural materials, and as electrical and thermal conductors.

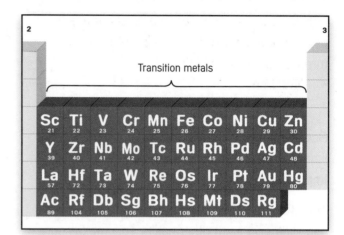

Extracting Metals

Titanium and **aluminium** are extracted from their ores by **electrolysis**. Electrolysis has many stages and requires a lot of energy, making it an expensive process.

Copper is useful for chemical wiring and plumbing.

Aluminium is resistant to corrosion and has a low density so it's very light.

Aluminium is used for drinks cans, window frames, lightweight vehicles and aeroplanes.

Titanium is strong and resistant to corrosion. It is used in aeroplanes, nuclear reactors and replacement hip joints.

Recycling Metals

Metals should be **recycled** wherever possible to...
- save money and energy
- make sure natural resources aren't used up
- reduce damage to the environment.

Quick Test

1. Complete the following sentence: Ores are mined and may be _____ before the metal is extracted and then _____ .
2. Iron is converted into steel by mixing iron with which element?
3. Copper can be extracted from low-grade ores by what two methods?
4. What is an alloy?
5. Why is pure iron soft and malleable?
6. Why are most metals in everyday use, e.g. copper and aluminium, mixed with small amounts of other metals?
7. What is the name of the block of metals in the middle of the Periodic Table?

Key Words   **Conductor**

Crude Oil

Crude oil on its own isn't very useful. But it is a **mixture** of a large number of compounds, some of which are very useful. Crude oil is a limited resource that is used to produce fuels and other chemicals.

A **mixture** consists of two or more elements or compounds that are **not chemically combined** together. The properties of the substances in a mixture remain unchanged, so they can be separated by physical methods, such as **distillation**.

Most of the compounds in crude oil consist of molecules made up of only **carbon** and **hydrogen** atoms. These compounds are called **hydrocarbons**. **Hydrocarbon** molecules vary in size, which affects their properties and how they are used as fuels.

The larger the hydrocarbon (i.e. the more carbon and hydrogen atoms in a molecule)…

- the less easily it flows (it's more viscous)
- the higher its boiling point
- the less volatile it is
- the less easily it ignites.

Long-chain Hydrocarbon

Short-chain Hydrocarbons

Fractional Distillation

Crude oil can be separated into different **fractions** (parts) by **fractional distillation.**

Each fraction contains hydrocarbon molecules with a similar number of carbon atoms. Most of the hydrocarbons obtained are **alkanes** (**saturated hydrocarbons**).

Fractionating Column

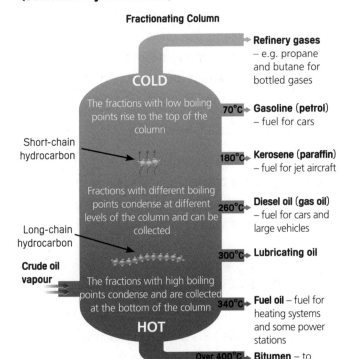

Ethanol and Hydrogen as Fuels

There are advantages and disadvantages to using ethanol and hydrogen as fuels.

Hydrogen as a biofuel	
Advantages	**Disdvantages**
• Water is the only product of combustion so it's a 'clean' fuel • Water is potentially a source of plentiful supplies of hydrogen	• There are currently no 'low energy' ways to extract hydrogen from water in large quantities • Hydrogen is a gas, so is difficult to store in large quantities • When hydrogen is mixed with air and ignited it's explosive, so there are safety issues to consider

Ethanol as a biofuel	
Advantages	**Disdvantages**
• A renewable energy source, i.e. helps to preserve fossil fuels • Sugar cane/beet (used to produce ethanol) grows quickly in countries with a hot climate, e.g. Brazil • Sugar cane/beet absorbs CO_2 from the atmosphere as it grows	• Sugar cane/beet can only be grown in countries with a hot climate • CO_2 is produced as a product of combustion (CO_2 is a greenhouse gas)

C1 Crude Oil and Fuels

Biofuels

Biofuels, e.g. biodiesel and ethanol, are fuels that are produced from plant material such as sugar.

The production and use of biofuels often have environmental advantages over traditional fuels.

Alkanes (Saturated Hydrocarbons)

The 'spine' of a hydrocarbon is made up of a chain of carbon atoms. When these chains are joined together by **single carbon–carbon bonds** the hydrocarbon is **saturated** and is known as an **alkane**.

- Hydrogen atoms can make one bond each.
- Carbon atoms can make four bonds each.
- The simplest alkane, **methane**, is made up of four hydrogen atoms and one carbon atom.

The general formula for alkanes is C_nH_{2n+2}

The carbon atoms in alkenes are linked to four other atoms by **single bonds**. This means that the alkane is saturated. This explains why alkanes are fairly unreactive, but they do burn well.

The shorter-chain hydrocarbons release energy more quickly by burning, so there is greater demand for them as **fuels**.

Alkanes can be represented as seen below. The '–' between atoms represents a covalent bond.

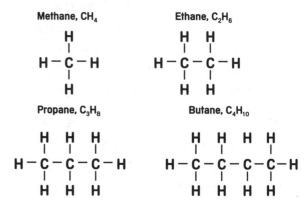

Burning Fuels

Most **fuels** contain carbon and hydrogen. Many also contain **sulfur**. As fuels burn they produce waste products, which are released into the atmosphere.

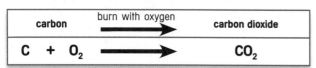

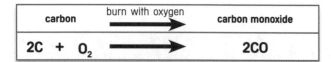

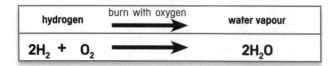

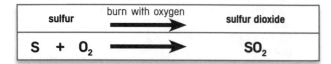

The combustion of hydrocarbon fuel releases energy. During combustion, both the carbon and hydrogen are oxidised. If combustion is not complete, then solid particles containing soot (carbon) and unburnt fuels may be released.

Due to the high temperature reached when fuels burn, nitrogen in the air can react with oxygen to form nitrogen oxides. These nitrogen oxides, like sulfur dioxide, can cause acid rain.

Carbon dioxide causes **global warming** due to the greenhouse effect. Solid particles in the air cause **global dimming**.

Sulfur can be removed from fuel before burning (e.g. in motor vehicles). Sulfur dioxide can be removed from the waste gases after **combustion** (e.g. in power stations). But both of these processes add to costs.

Biofuel • Saturated • Alkane • Fuel

Other Useful Substances from Crude Oil C1

Cracking Hydrocarbons

Longer-chain hydrocarbons can be broken down into shorter, more useful hydrocarbons. This process is called **cracking**.

Long-chain hydrocarbon → (heat + catalyst) → Short-chain hydrocarbons

Cracking involves...
- heating the hydrocarbons until they vaporise
- passing the vapour over a hot **catalyst** (or mixed with steam).

A **thermal decomposition** reaction then takes place.

The products of cracking include **alkanes** and **alkenes** (**unsaturated** **hydrocarbons**). Some of the products are useful as fuels. Alkenes react with bromine water, turning it from orange to colourless.

Cracking Hydrocarbons in the Laboratory

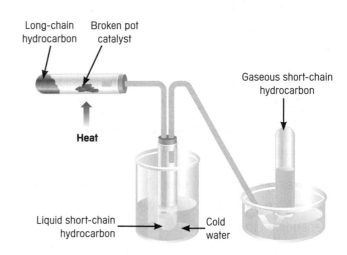

Alkenes (Unsaturated Hydrocarbons)

As well as forming single bonds with other atoms, carbon atoms can form **double bonds**. This means that not all the carbon atoms are linked to four other atoms; a **double carbon–carbon bond** is present instead.

Some of the products of cracking are hydrocarbon molecules with at least one double bond (**alkenes**).
- The general formula for alkenes is C_nH_{2n}
- The simplest alkene is ethene, C_2H_4

- Ethene is made up of four hydrogen atoms and two carbon atoms, and contains one double carbon–carbon bond.

Alkenes can be represented using displayed formulae:

Ethene, C_2H_4 Propene, C_3H_6

Double bond

Making Alcohol from Ethene

Ethanol is an alcohol. It can be produced by reacting the alkene **ethene** with steam in the presence of a **catalyst**, phosphoric acid.

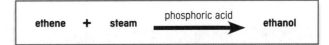

ethene + steam → (phosphoric acid) → ethanol

Making Alcohol by Fermentation

Ethanol can be produced by the **fermentation** of sugar, which is a renewable resource. During fermentation, sugar is converted into ethanol and carbon dioxide.

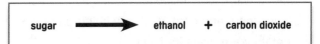

sugar → ethanol + carbon dioxide

Polymerisation

Because alkenes are unsaturated (i.e. they contain a double bond), they are useful for making other molecules, especially **polymers** (long-chain molecules).

Many small alkene molecules (monomers) join together to form polymers. This is **polymerisation**.

Polymers such as **poly(ethene)** and **poly(propene)** are made in this way.

For example, slime with different **viscosities** can be made from poly(ethenol). The viscosity of the slime depends on the temperature and concentrations of the poly(ethenol) and borax from which it is made.

The materials commonly called **plastics** are all synthetic polymers.

The small alkene molecules are called monomers.

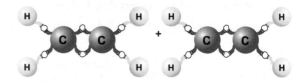

Their double bonds are easily broken.

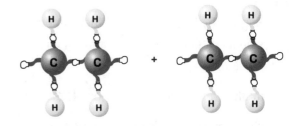

Large numbers of molecules can therefore be joined in this way.

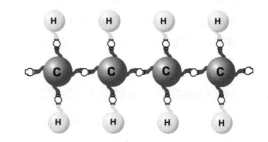

Representing Polymerisation

Polymerisation can be represented like this:

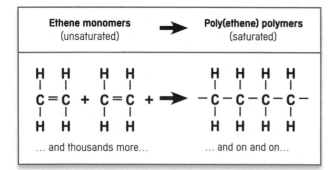

The general formula for polymerisation can be used to represent the formation of any simple polymer:

where n is a very large number

Biodegradable Polymers

Many polymers are not **biodegradable**, so they are not broken down by microbes. This can lead to problems with waste disposal. Plastic bags made from polymers and cornstarch are being produced so that they are biodegradable.

Other Useful Substances from Crude Oil C1

Polymers

Polymers have many useful applications and new uses are being developed. Polymers and composites are widely used in medicine and dentistry. For example…

- implantable materials are used for tissue surgery
- hard-wearing anti-bacterial dental cements, coating and fillers are used in dentistry
- hydrogels can be used as wound dressings.

Polymers can also be used to coat fabrics with a waterproof layer.

Smart materials, including shape-memory polymers, are also increasingly more common.

Specific polymers can have different uses, for example…

- polyvinyl chloride (PVC) is used to make waterproof items and drain pipes, and can be used as an electrical insulator
- polystyrene is used to make the casing for electrical appliances, and it can be expanded to make protective packaging
- poly(ethene) is used to make plastic bags and bottles
- poly(propene) is used to make crates and ropes.

Disposing of Plastics

Plastic is a versatile material. It's cheap and easy to produce, but this means a lot of plastic waste is generated.

There are various ways of **disposing of plastics**. Unfortunately some of them have an impact on the environment.

Burning plastics produces air **pollution**. Burning releases carbon dioxide, which contributes to **global warming**.

Some plastics can't be burned at all because they produce toxic fumes.

Plastics can be dumped in **landfill sites**. But most plastics are **non-biodegradable**. This means that microorganisms have no effect on them, so they will not **decompose** and rot away. The use of landfill sites means that plastic waste builds up.

Research is currently being carried out on the development of **biodegradable plastics**.

Quick Test

1. Which two chemical elements make up most of the molecules in crude oil?
2. What is the name of the process by which crude oil is separated?
3. Name two gases that may be released into the atmosphere when a fuel burns.
4. What are the major environmental concerns over releasing carbon dioxide and sulfur dioxide into the atmosphere?
5. What name is given to the process by which hydrocarbons are broken down into smaller, more useful molecules?
6. What name is given to unsaturated hydrocarbons?
7. What is the chemical test for alkenes?
8. What name is given to the small molecules that join together to form polymers?

C1 Plant Oils and their Uses

Getting Oil from Plants

Many plants produce fruit, seeds and nuts that are rich in **oils.**

The oil can be extracted from plant materials by pressing (crushing) them or by **distillation**. These processes remove the water and other impurities from the plant material.

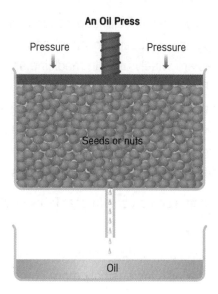

An Oil Press

Pressure   Pressure

Seeds or nuts

Oil

Vegetable Oils

Vegetable oils are important foods. These oils provide you with nutrients and energy. Vegetable oils can also be used as a **fuel** in converted vehicles, instead of petrol or diesel.

Vegetable oils contain **double carbon–carbon bonds**, so they are **unsaturated**. They can be detected using **bromine water**. Unsaturated fats (oils) **decolourise bromine water**. Vegetable oils are used in cooking because they have a higher boiling point than water so can be used to cook foods at higher temperatures. This means that food can be cooked more quickly and a different flavour is added to food.

Cooking using vegetable oil also increases the energy that food releases when it is eaten.

Cooking with oils higher in unsaturated fats is believed to be healthier than cooking with saturated fats.

HT Use of Vegetable Oils in Cooking

Generally, the more double carbon–carbon bonds there are in a substance, the lower its melting point.

So, **unsaturated fats** (oils) tend to have melting points below room temperature.

The melting point of an oil can be raised above room temperature by removing some or all of its carbon–carbon bonds. This hardens the oil into a solid fat, for example margarine, which can be spread on bread or used for making cakes and pastries.

This hardening process is called **hydrogenation**.

1 The **unsaturated fat (oil)** is heated with **hydrogen** at about 60°C, in the presence of a **nickel catalyst**.

2 A reaction takes place that **removes** the double carbon–carbon bonds to produce a **saturated fat** (**hydrogenated oil**). Removing more double bonds makes the saturated fat harder.

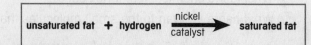

unsaturated fat + hydrogen $\xrightarrow[\text{catalyst}]{\text{nickel}}$ saturated fat

Emulsions

Oils don't dissolve in water, but an oil can be mixed with water to produce an **emulsion**.

Emulsions are thicker than oil or water and have a…
- better texture
- better appearance
- better coating ability.

Emulsions have many uses, for example in…
- salad dressings
- ice cream
- cosmetics
- paints

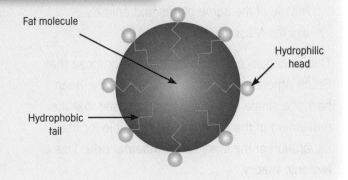

HT Hydrophobic and Hydrophilic Properties of Emulsifiers

An **emulsifier** is a substance that helps to stabilise an emulsion. Emulsifier molecules have a…
- **hydrophilic** (water loving) head that mixes with water molecules
- **hydrophobic** (water hating) tail that mixes with oil molecules.

This allows water and oils to mix.

Fat molecule

Hydrophilic head

Hydrophobic tail

Quick Test

1. Why are vegetable oils important foods?
2. Why can vegetable oils be used to cook foods at higher temperatures than water?
3. Give two uses of emulsions.
4. What kind of bond do unsaturated vegetable oils contain?

C1 Changes in the Earth and its Atmosphere

Structure of the Earth

The **Earth** is nearly spherical. It has a layered structure that consists of…

- a thin **crust**
- a **mantle**
- a **core** (made of nickel and iron).

Rocks at the Earth's surface are continually being broken up, reformed and changed in an ongoing cycle of events, known as the **rock cycle**. The changes take a very long time.

Crust – 10–100km thick

Core – has liquid outer part and solid inner part

Mantle – has properties of a solid but flows very slowly

Tectonic Theory

At one time, scientists believed that features on the Earth's surface, e.g. mountain ranges, were caused by shrinkage of the crust when the Earth cooled down following its formation.

But as scientists have found out more about the Earth this **theory** has been rejected.

Evidence showed scientists that the east coast of South America and the west coast of Africa have…

- **closely matching coastlines**
- **similar patterns of rocks**, which contain **fossils** of the same plants and animals, e.g. the Mesosaurus.

This evidence led Alfred Wegener to propose that South America and Africa had at one time been part of a single land mass. He proposed that the movement of the crust was responsible for the separation of the land, i.e. **continental drift**. This is **tectonic theory**.

Unfortunately, Wegener couldn't explain **how** the crust moved. It took more than 50 years for scientists to discover this.

South America and Africa Now

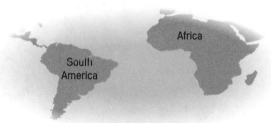

Africa

South America

How South America and Africa Could Have Looked

Africa

South America

How the Earth Once Was

Laurasia

Gondwanaland

How the Earth Is Today

Key Words Theory • Evidence • Fossil

Tectonic Plates

The Earth's lithosphere (the crust and the upper part of the mantle) is 'cracked' into **tectonic plates**.

Intense heat, released by radioactive decay deep in the Earth, creates convection currents in the mantle. These currents cause the tectonic plates to move apart very slowly, a few centimetres per year.

In convection in a gas or a liquid, the matter rises as it is heated. As it gets further away from the heat source, it cools and sinks. The same happens in the Earth:

1 Hot molten rock rises to the surface, creating new crust.

2 The older, cooler crust, then sinks down where the **convection current** starts to fall.

3 The land masses on these plates move slowly.

The movements are usually small and gradual. But sometimes they can be sudden and disastrous. **Earthquakes** and **volcanic eruptions** are common occurrences at plate boundaries. They are hard to predict.

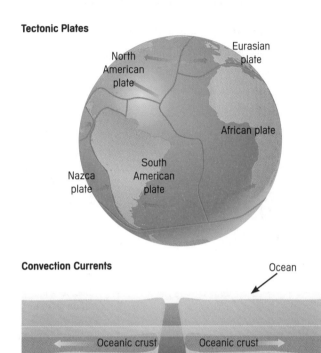

Tectonic Plates

North American plate · Eurasian plate · African plate · Nazca plate · South American plate

Convection Currents

Ocean · Oceanic crust · Oceanic crust · Convection currents in the mantle · Convection currents in the mantle · Hot molten rock

The Origin of Life

There are many theories as to how life on Earth was formed because there is little direct evidence and therefore a number of assumptions have to be made.

(HT) Two scientists, **Miller** and **Urey**, tried to test one possible theory for how life on Earth began. They mixed together the chemicals thought to be present in the Earth's early atmosphere – water, methane and ammonia. The mixture was heated and sparks (electrical discharges) to represent ultraviolet radiation from the Sun were passed through it. The mixture was cooled and the cycle repeated many times.

After many cycles the mixture contained simple organic molecules, like amino acids, that are the building blocks of living organisms. This is known as the **primordial soup theory**, which is one (of many) that offers an explanation for how life began.

Quick Test

1 Complete the following sentences.

a) The Earth consists of a core, _____ and _____ .

b) Convection currents within the Earth's mantle cause the crust's plates to _____ slowly.

c) Earthquakes and/or volcanoes can occur at the boundaries between _____ _____ .

Key Words   **Tectonic plates**

The Atmosphere

The **atmosphere** has changed a lot since the formation of the Earth 4.6 billion years ago.

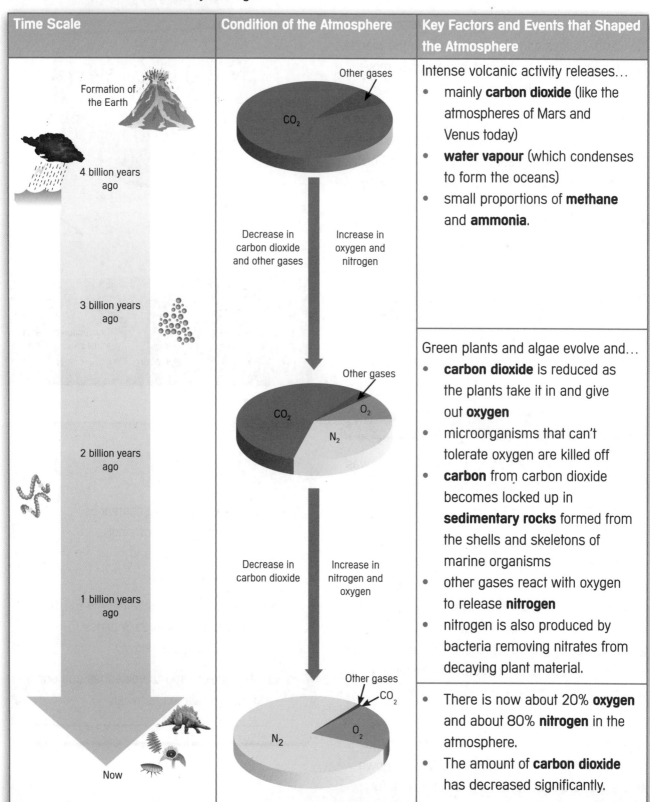

Time Scale	Condition of the Atmosphere	Key Factors and Events that Shaped the Atmosphere
Formation of the Earth 4 billion years ago 3 billion years ago 2 billion years ago 1 billion years ago Now	Other gases CO_2 Decrease in carbon dioxide and other gases / Increase in oxygen and nitrogen Other gases CO_2 O_2 N_2 Decrease in carbon dioxide / Increase in nitrogen and oxygen Other gases CO_2 N_2 O_2	Intense volcanic activity releases... • mainly **carbon dioxide** (like the atmospheres of Mars and Venus today) • **water vapour** (which condenses to form the oceans) • small proportions of **methane** and **ammonia**.
		Green plants and algae evolve and... • **carbon dioxide** is reduced as the plants take it in and give out **oxygen** • microorganisms that can't tolerate oxygen are killed off • **carbon** from carbon dioxide becomes locked up in **sedimentary rocks** formed from the shells and skeletons of marine organisms • other gases react with oxygen to release **nitrogen** • nitrogen is also produced by bacteria removing nitrates from decaying plant material.
		• There is now about 20% **oxygen** and about 80% **nitrogen** in the atmosphere. • The amount of **carbon dioxide** has decreased significantly.

Changes in the Earth and its Atmosphere C1

Composition of the Atmosphere

The proportions of gases in the atmosphere have been more or less the same for about 200 million years. The proportions are shown in the pie chart. **Water vapour** may also be present in varying quantities (0–3%).

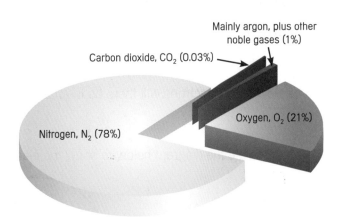

Mainly argon, plus other noble gases (1%)

Carbon dioxide, CO_2 (0.03%)

Oxygen, O_2 (21%)

Nitrogen, N_2 (78%)

Changes in the Atmosphere

The level of carbon dioxide in the atmosphere today is increasing due to...

- **volcanic activity** – geological activity moves carbonate rocks deep into the Earth and during volcanic activity they may release carbon dioxide back into the atmosphere
- **the burning of fossil fuels** – burning carbon, which has been locked up in **fossil fuels** for millions of years, releases carbon dioxide into the atmosphere.

The level of carbon dioxide in the atmosphere is reduced by the reaction between carbon dioxide and sea water. This reaction produces...

- insoluble carbonates that are deposited as sediment
- soluble hydrogencarbonates.

But too much carbon dioxide dissolving in the oceans can harm marine life.

The carbonates form some of the **sedimentary rocks** in the Earth's crust.

HT Fractional Distillation of Liquid Air

Air is a mixture of gases with different boiling points. The different gases can be collected by cooling air to a liquid and then heating it.

These gases are used as raw materials in a variety of industrial processes.

Nitrogen   Oxygen   Carbon Dioxide

Quick Test

1. a) Which two gases is the atmosphere mainly made up of?
   b) Name one other gas present in the atmosphere.
2. How is oxygen thought to have been released into the atmosphere?
3. What are the two main ways that carbon dioxide is absorbed from the Atmosphere?

1 This question is about sodium and oxygen. Sodium is a metal and oxygen is a non-metal. An atom of sodium contains 11 protons and an atom of oxygen contains 8 protons.

a) What charge do protons have?

.... **(1 mark)**

b) How many electrons will there be in an atom of sodium?

.... **(1 mark)**

c) Complete the diagram below to show the electronic structure of an atom of sodium. **(1 mark)**

d) When sodium and oxygen react together sodium oxide is formed, which has the chemical formula Na_2O.

i) Complete the following sentence.

Na_2O contains a total of .... atoms. **(1 mark)**

(HT) **ii)** Balance the equation below showing the formation of sodium oxide from sodium and oxygen.

$$Na + O_2 \longrightarrow Na_2O$$ **(1 mark)**

2 This question concerns some of the reactions of limestone. Limestone contains calcium carbonate ($CaCO_3$).

Limestone can be decomposed upon heating to form calcium oxide and carbon dioxide. Calcium oxide reacts with water to form calcium hydroxide. Calcium hydroxide solution is commonly known as limewater.

a) How is limestone obtained from the earth?

.... **(1 mark)**

b) Name another metal carbonate that decomposes upon heating in the same way as limestone.

.... **(1 mark)**

c) What would you observe if carbon dioxide gas is bubbled through limewater?

.... **(1 mark)**

3 Copper is a very useful metal that is mined and extracted from ores. Some ores are copper-rich. Other low-grade ores contain less copper. Copper can be used for electrical wiring.

a) Explain why copper is a useful material for use in electrical wiring.

.... **(1 mark)**

b) How is copper extracted from copper-rich ores?

.... **(1 mark)**

c) How is this copper then purified?

.... **(1 mark)**

d) Name one method used to extract copper from low-grade ores.

.... **(1 mark)**

4 Crude oil is a mixture of a large number of compounds. Many of these compounds are hydrocarbons. The combustion of hydrocarbon fuels releases heat but also many pollutant gases.

a) What do you understand by the term **mixture**?

.... **(1 mark)**

b) Which two elements do hydrocarbon compounds contain?

.... **(2 marks)**

c) Name a gas that may be released into the atmosphere when a hydrocarbon fuel burns.

.... **(1 mark)**

d) What name is given to the process of converting long-chain hydrocarbons into smaller, more useful molecules?

.... **(1 mark)**

5 Consider the two molecules (labelled as X and Y) shown below:

$$
X \qquad
\begin{array}{ccc}
 & H & H \\
 & | & | \\
H - & C - C & - H \\
 & | & | \\
 & H & H
\end{array}
\qquad\qquad
Y \qquad
\begin{array}{c}
H \quad\quad H \\
\diagdown \quad\quad \diagup \\
C = C \\
\diagup \quad\quad \diagdown \\
H \quad\quad H
\end{array}
$$

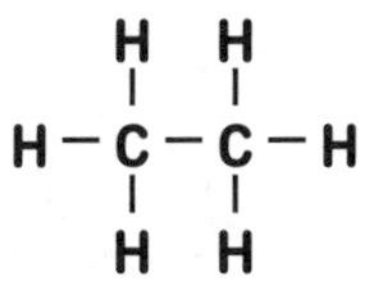

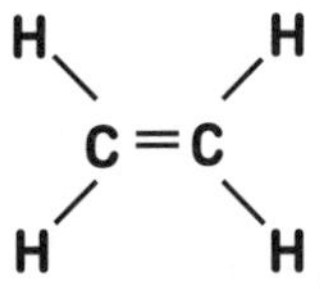

Which molecule, X or Y, is...

a) Saturated ....

b) An alkene ....

c) Used to make polymers ....

d) Able to decolourise bromine water ....

(4 marks)

P1 Energy Transfer

Infrared Radiation

Infrared radiation involves the transfer of **heat energy** by electromagnetic radiation, also called **thermal radiation**. No particles of matter are involved in the process.

All objects emit and absorb infrared radiation.

The hotter an object is the more infrared radiation it radiates.

The amount of infrared radiation an object gives out or takes in depends on its **surface**, **shape** and **dimensions**.

An object will emit and absorb infrared radiation faster if there's a bigger difference in temperature between it and its surroundings. Different materials transfer thermal energy at different rates.

At the same temperature dark, matt surfaces…
- emit more infrared radiation than light, shiny surfaces
- absorb more infrared radiation than light, shiny surfaces.

Light, shiny surfaces are good reflectors of infrared radiation. An example of a good reflector is the 'silvering' on the inside of a vacuum flask.

Kinetic Theory

Kinetic theory explains the different **states** and **properties** of **matter** in terms of the movement of the millions and millions of particles (atoms / molecules). The particles of gases, liquids and solids have different amounts of energy.

The atoms / molecules that make up a gas are always moving. **They move very quickly** in **random directions**, colliding with each other and with the walls of the container they are in.

When the temperature increases…
- the gas molecules move faster
- the collisions become more intense.

When the temperature falls…
- the gas molecules move more slowly
- the molecules move closer together
- the collisions become less frequent
- the gas begins to form a liquid.

Eventually the liquid becomes a solid. The atoms / molecules in a solid can only move (**vibrate**) about a **fixed position**, so they form a **regular** and **orderly pattern**.

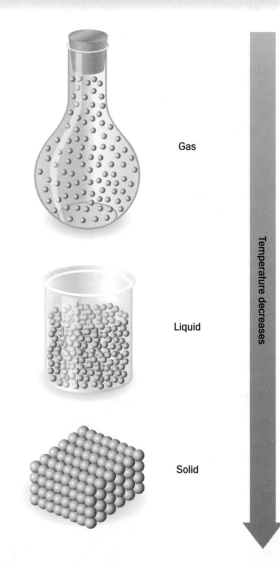

Gas

Liquid

Solid

Temperature decreases

     Infrared radiation • Thermal radiation • Kinetic theory

Energy Transfer by Heating

Energy transfer by heating involves the movement of particles. This can be undertaken by a variety of mechanisms including…

- conduction
- convection
- evaporation
- condensation.

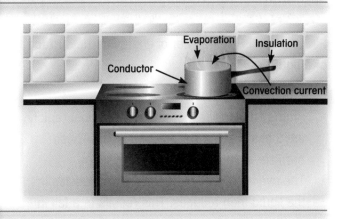

Conduction

Conduction is the transfer of energy by heating without the substance itself moving. For example, metals are good **conductors** of energy:

- As a metal becomes hotter the **atoms vibrate** more vigorously.
- This additional energy is transferred to the cooler parts of the metal by the **free electrons** that roam throughout the metal.

Insulators are materials that have few or no free electrons, so they can't readily transfer their energy by heating.

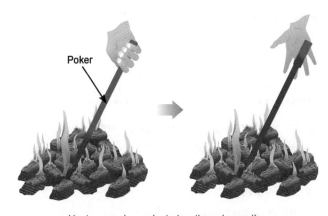

Heat energy is conducted up the poker as the hotter parts transfer energy to the colder parts

Convection

Convection is the transfer of energy by heating through the movement of particles.

Convection occurs in liquids and gases, creating **convection currents**:

1. Particles in the liquid or gas nearest the energy source move **faster**, causing the substance to **expand** and become **less dense**.
2. The warm liquid or gas now rises vertically. As it does so it **cools**, becomes **denser** and eventually sinks.
3. The colder, denser liquid or gas moves into the space created (close to the heat source) and the cycle repeats.

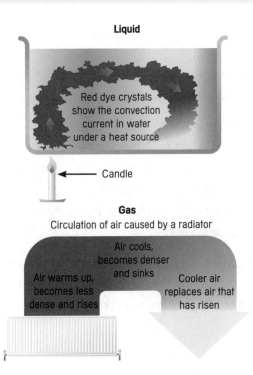

Liquid

Red dye crystals show the convection current in water under a heat source

Candle

Gas
Circulation of air caused by a radiator

Air cools, becomes denser and sinks

Air warms up, becomes less dense and rises

Cooler air replaces air that has risen

P1 Energy Transfer

Evaporation and Condensation

Evaporation is the transfer of energy at the **surface of a liquid**.

In terms of kinetic theory:

- Atoms / molecules that are moving most rapidly are located at the surface of a liquid. These particles behave like a gas and escape.
- The overall energy of the atoms / molecules in the liquid then reduces. This results in a fall in its temperature, i.e. it cools.

When water evaporates from a surface, it becomes a gas called **water vapour**.

The opposite effect, where the gas or vapour returns to a liquid state at the surface, is called **condensation**. This transfers energy back into the substance at the surface.

Water evaporates quickly when it's hotter. As the water boils, it turns into steam

Rate of Energy Transfer

Under similar conditions different materials will transfer energy by heating at very **different rates**. The rate at which a material transfers energy depends on…

- its **surface area** and **volume**
- the **type** of material it's made from
- the **nature** of the surface with which the material is in contact
- its temperature.

For example…

- cooling fins on a motorbike engine allow the transfer of energy from the engine to the surrounding air a lot faster
- a desert fox has far larger ears than an Arctic fox to allow for a more efficient way of getting rid of unwanted energy.

The **bigger** the **temperature difference** between an object and its surroundings, the **faster** the rate at which energy is transferred.

Heating and Insulating Buildings

Architects are able to calculate the amount of energy that is lost from buildings by using **U-values**:

- U-values give a measure of how effective a particular material is as an insulator.
- The **lower** the U-value the **better** the material is as an **insulator**.

Solar panels may contain water that is heated by radiation from the Sun. This water can then be used to **heat buildings** or provide **domestic hot water**.

Using Solar Energy / Radiation to Heat Water

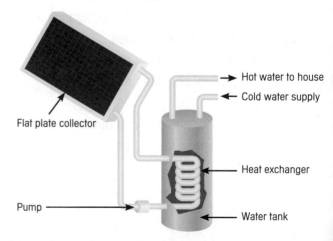

Flat plate collector

Hot water to house
Cold water supply
Heat exchanger
Pump
Water tank

Specific Heat Capacity

Different materials (with identical masses and at the same temperature) can store different amounts of energy.

The quantity known as the **specific heat capacity** is the amount of energy required to change the temperature of 1kg of a material by 1°C.

To work out the energy required use the following equation:

$$E = m \times c \times \theta$$

where E is the energy transferred in joules (J)
m is the mass (kg)
c is the specific heat capacity that has units of J / kg °C
θ is the temperature change (°C)

For example, the specific heat capacity of water is 4200J / kg^{-1} °C

To compare against water, the table below shows the specific heat capacity of various materials.

Material	Specific heat capacity (J / kg°C)
Air	1012
Aluminium	897
Copper	385
Petrol	2220

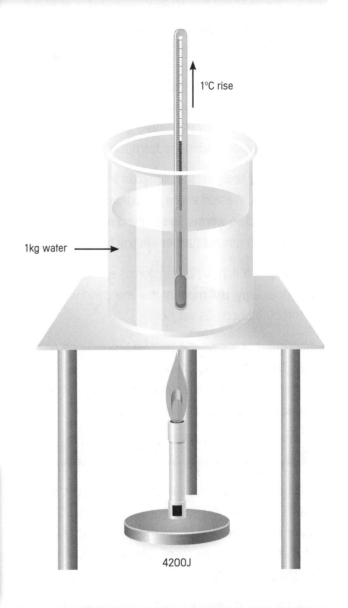

1°C rise

1kg water

4200J

Quick Test

1. What type of radiation do all objects emit?
2. Is the following statement true or false? 'Light, shiny surfaces are good reflectors and poor emitters of infrared radiation.'
3. When a pure solid metal is made, what patterns do the metallic atoms take?
4. What is responsible for metals behaving as good conductors?
5. Give the two main factors that affect the rate of evaporation or condensation.
6. What does the U-value measure?
7. Calculate the energy transferred when 0.1kg of water at 0°C is brought to boiling point (i.e. 100°C). (N.B. the specific heat capacity of water is 4200 J / kg°C.)

Energy Transfers

Energy can be **transferred, usually stored**, or **dissipated**, but it can't be **created** or **destroyed**.

Many devices take in energy in one form and transfer the energy into another form. In doing so only part of the energy is usefully transferred to where it's wanted and in the form that's wanted.

The remaining energy is transferred in a **non-useful way**, i.e. is **wasted**. Wasted energy becomes increasingly spread out and so **warms its surroundings**. In this form it is difficult to use for further energy transfers.

For example, a light bulb transforms electrical energy into light energy. But most of the energy is wasted and the bulb becomes very hot.

A diagram that shows the relative proportions of energy transfers using arrows is called a **Sankey diagram**. The **widths of arrows** are proportional to the **amount of energy** they represent.

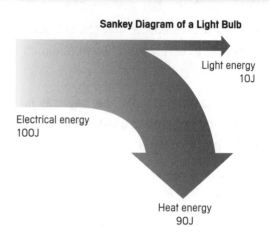

Sankey Diagram of a Light Bulb

Light energy
10J

Electrical energy
100J

Heat energy
90J

Electrical appliances transfer energy for different uses, and some of the energy is wasted:

- A kettle transfers energy in the form of heat (to the water), but energy is also wasted as heat (to the kettle and air) and as sound.
- An electric motor (e.g. drill, washing machine) transfers kinetic energy, but energy is also wasted in the form of heat and sound.

Energy Efficiency

The **efficiency** of a device refers to the proportion of energy (or power) that is usefully transferred. **The greater the proportion** of energy (power) that is usefully transferred, the more efficient and the more **cost-effective** the device is.

Replacing an old television with a more energy efficient one may cost £600, but may also provide an annual saving of £60 per year. The **pay-back time** can be calculated as $\dfrac{£600}{£60 \text{ per year}} = 10$ years

Efficiency values are usually expressed either as a **percentage** or as a **decimal** number. Efficiency can be calculated using the following equation:

$$\text{Efficiency} = \frac{\text{Useful energy or useful power out}}{\text{Total energy or total power in}} \times 100\%$$

For example, only a quarter of the energy supplied to a television is usefully transferred into light and sound. The rest is wasted, so it's only 0.25 or 25% efficient.

Transferring Electrical Energy

Most of the energy transferred to houses and industry is in the form of **electrical energy**.

Electrical energy is easily transferred…
- by heaters to heat surroundings, e.g. a hairdryer
- into light energy, e.g. a lamp
- into sound energy, e.g. stereo speakers
- into kinetic energy (movement), e.g. an electric fan.

The amount of energy transferred by an electrical appliance depends on…
- **how long** the appliance is switched on
- **how fast** (the rate of energy transfer) the appliance transfers energy, i.e. its **power**.

Without a reliable source of electrical energy we could have power cuts – creating the need to use candles for lighting and leaving many people without heating or cooking facilities.

Energy Calculations

Energy is normally measured in **joules (J)**. **Power** gives a measure of the rate of energy transfer. The power of an appliance is measured in **watts** (W) or sometimes for bigger amounts, **kilowatts** (kW). 1 watt is the same as 1 joule per second (J/s).

To calculate the amount of energy transferred from the mains, the following equation can be used:

$$E = P \times t$$	where E is the energy transferred, P is the power of the appliance and t is the time

In terms of units:
- Energy transferred (in joules) = power (in watts) x time (seconds).
- Energy transferred (in kilowatt-hours) = power (kilowatts) x time (hours).

To calculate the cost of mains electricity or energy transferred by the mains for an appliance, use the following equation:

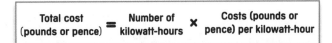

| Total cost (pounds or pence) | = | Number of kilowatt-hours | x | Costs (pounds or pence) per kilowatt-hour |

Example

Electricity Statement for the 3rd quarter (3 months).

Present reading	Previous reading	kWh used	Cost per kWh (p)	Charge amount (£)
30803	30332	471	9.45	44.51

kWh calculated by subtracting present reading from previous reading

kWh x cost per kWh
$471 \times \dfrac{9.45}{100} = £44.51$

Quick Test

1. When energy is transferred part of it may be useful. What happens to the rest?
2. A small wind turbine requires 2000J of energy from the wind but only provides 250J of useful electrical energy. What is the efficiency of the turbine as a percentage?
3. What is a Sankey diagram?
4. What are the units of **a)** electrical energy and **b)** power?
5. The amount of electrical energy transferred by a very bright light bulb is 200 joules per second. What is the power rating of the bulb?
6. A washing machine with a power consumption of 1600W is on for 45 minutes. Calculate **a)** the amount of energy transferred in kWh **b)** the total cost assuming the unit cost is 10p per kilowatt-hour.

Generating Electricity

In some power stations an energy source is used to heat water. The steam produced drives a turbine that is connected to an electrical generator. The different types of energy sources used include…

- **fossil fuels**, e.g. coal, oil and gas, which are burned to heat water or air
- **nuclear fuels**, e.g. uranium and plutonium, in which nuclear fission is used to heat water
- **biofuels**, e.g. wood or methane, which can be burned to heat water.

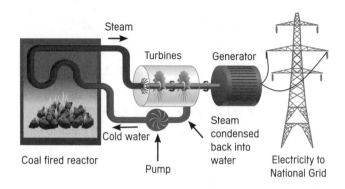

Steam · Turbines · Generator · Steam condensed back into water · Electricity to National Grid · Cold water · Pump · Coal fired reactor

Non-renewable Energy Sources

We depend on **non-renewable energy sources** (e.g. coal, oil, gas and nuclear) for most of our energy needs. They can't be replaced within a lifetime, so they will eventually run out.

Source	Advantages	Disadvantages	Start-up time
Nuclear	• Cost of fuel is low • Rate of fuel use is low • Doesn't produce CO_2 and SO_2 emissions into the atmosphere	• Radioactive waste produced • Difficulty of storing radioactive material for thousands of years • Building new power stations is very costly • Decommissioning is very costly • Accident and radioactive contamination risks are high	Longest
Coal	• Relatively cheap and easy to extract	• Burning coal produces CO_2 (**Greenhouse effect**) and SO_2 (**acid rain**) emissions into the atmosphere • Perhaps only several hundred years of coal left	
Oil	• Has been relatively easy to find • Perhaps large amounts of reserve stocks available	• Burning produces CO_2 and SO_2 emissions into the atmosphere • Significant risk of spillage and pollution • Destruction of wildlife habitats	
Gas	• Has been relatively easy to find • Perhaps large amounts of reserve stocks available • Doesn't produce SO_2 emissions into the atmosphere	• Burning produces CO_2 emissions into the atmosphere (although less than coal or oil) • Expensive pipelines and networks are required • Visual pollution of landscape • Destruction of wildlife habitats	Shortest

Renewable Energy Sources

Renewable energy sources will not run out because they are continually being replaced. Most renewable energy sources are caused by the Sun or Moon.

The Sun causes…
* evaporation, which results in rain and flowing water
* convection currents, which result in winds that create waves.

The gravitational pull of the Moon creates tides.

Renewable energy sources can be used directly to drive turbines and generators. New sources include **biofuels**, which can be solid, liquid or gas. Biofuels are obtained from lifeless or living biological material. Biofuels include…
* liquid ethanol (derived from fermented plant material such as sugar cane)
* methane gas (from sludge digesters)
* straw, nutshells and woodchip.

Source	Advantages	Disadvantages
Wind turbines	• No fuel and little maintenance • No polluting gases produced • Can be built offshore	• Land-based turbines give visual and noise pollution • High initial capital building costs • Not very flexible in meeting demand • Variation in wind affects output
Tidal and waves	• No fuel required • No polluting gases produced • Barrage water can be released when demand is high	• Visual pollution and hazard to shipping • Can destroy / alter wildlife habitats • Variations in tides / waves affects output • Very high capital costs to build them
Hydroelectric	• Fast start-up time • No polluting gases produced • Water can be pumped back to the reservoir when demand is low	• Involves damming upland valleys • Destruction of wildlife habitats • Need an adequate rainfall • Very high initial costs
Solar cells	• Uses light from the Sun • Useful in remote locations • No polluting gases emitted • Small-scale production possible	• Depends on light intensity • Use of high cost semiconductor materials • Efficiency is poor • Visual pollution of large areas of solar panels
Biofuels	• Flexible product • Cost effective • Little impact on the environment	• Some pre-processing of the material is required • Limited resources due to land area requirements
Geothermal	• No pollutants produced • Uses naturally occurring hot water and steam directly • Low start-up costs	• Restricted to only certain volcanic areas • Subsidence risk

Often small-scale productions can be set-up and built locally to provide electricity, e.g. solar cells for homes and roadside signs. Although these tend to be uneconomical to connect to, and support, the National Grid, this is now changing following a much larger increase in the number of small-scale productions being used in the UK.

Key Words   Renewable energy source

P1 Methods We Use to Generate Electricity

Carbon Capture

A recent and rapidly expanding technology is the capture and storage of carbon dioxide. Capturing CO_2 and reducing its effect in the atmosphere is vitally important in reducing the effects of global warming.

Storing CO_2 in natural containers, such as the old oil and gas fields under the North Sea, is one solution being proposed.

The National Grid

Electricity that is generated in power stations is transferred to homes, schools and industry by the **National Grid**.

Whilst overhead power lines are visually polluting they are more reliable and relatively easy to maintain compared with power cables underground, which are very costly to install.

Transformers are used to change the **potential difference** (voltage) of the **alternating current** (a.c.) supply before and after it is transmitted through the National Grid. Both **step-up** and **step-down** transformers are used.

Increasing the potential difference reduces the current required for a given power. This reduction in current reduces the energy losses in the cables when electricity is transferred to consumers.

- **Step-up transformers** increase the potential difference (400 000 volts) allowing power lines to transmit electricity from the power station with reduced energy loss.
- **Step-down transformers** decrease the potential difference (230 volts) and increase the current before it is used by consumers.

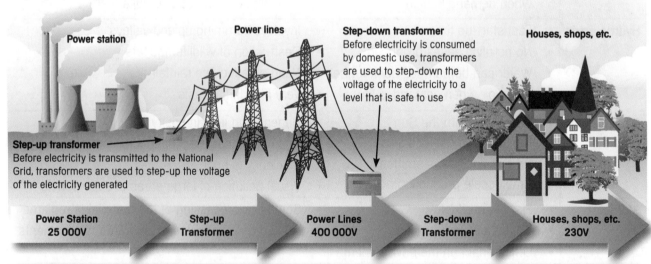

Power station

Power lines

Step-down transformer
Before electricity is consumed by domestic use, transformers are used to step-down the voltage of the electricity to a level that is safe to use

Houses, shops, etc.

Step-up transformer
Before electricity is transmitted to the National Grid, transformers are used to step-up the voltage of the electricity generated

| Power Station 25 000V | Step-up Transformer | Power Lines 400 000V | Step-down Transformer | Houses, shops, etc. 230V |

Quick Test

1. Give two examples of fossil fuels.
2. What is a biofuel?
3. Give one advantage and one disadvantage of solar power.
4. A rapidly evolving technology involves carbon capture. Why is this important and where will it be stored?
5. Why is the potential difference in overhead transmission cables 400 000V?
6. What is the function of a step-down transformer?

Key Words   **National Grid • Transformer • Potential difference**

Properties of Waves

There are two types of wave:

- A transverse wave is where the oscillations are **perpendicular** to the direction of energy transfer, e.g. electromagnetic waves and water waves.
- A longitudinal wave is where the oscillations are **parallel** to the direction of energy transfer, e.g. sound waves. These waves show areas of **compression** and **rarefaction**.

All waves transfer energy. **Mechanical waves** (e.g. water waves, waves on springs and shock waves) may be transverse or longitudinal.

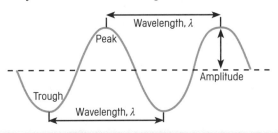

Electromagnetic Spectrum

The electromagnetic spectrum extends from high frequency or high energy (**short wavelength 10^{-15}m**) waves, e.g. gamma rays, to low frequency or low energy (**long wavelength 10^4m**) waves, e.g. **radio waves**.

Visible light is one type of electromagnetic radiation and is the only part of the electromagnetic spectrum that can be seen with the eye. It consists of seven primary bands of colour from **red to violet**.

All waves can be described in terms of their amplitude, frequency and **wavelength**. The wavelength is simply the distance between two successive peaks or troughs in a wave.

The Electromagnetic Spectrum

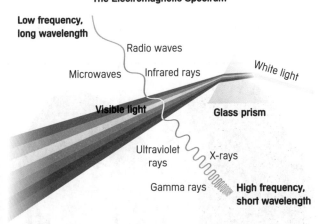

The amplitude of an electromagnetic wave is the peak movement of the wave from its rest point. The frequency of an electromagnetic wave is the number of waves passing in one second. Frequency is measured in hertz (Hz).

The connection between frequency and wavelength is given by the wave equation:

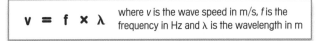

$$v = f \times \lambda$$

where v is the wave speed in m/s, f is the frequency in Hz and λ is the wavelength in m

Waves can be **reflected** and **refracted** when they meet a surface (interface). Transverse and longitudinal waves can also be **diffracted**, for example...

- water waves entering harbours
- radio waves diffracted by hills and large buildings.

When waves are refracted at a surface they undergo a change of direction, except when they are directed at the surface along the **normal**.

Communication

Different parts of the electromagnetic spectrum can be used for communication.

Electromagnetic Waves	Uses
Radio waves	• Television and radio signals allow communication across the Earth
Microwaves	• Mobile phone networks and satellite communication (although there are potential risks of using mobile phones, e.g. possible links with brain tumours) • Cooking – water molecules absorb microwaves and heat up
Infrared	• Remote controls for televisions, etc. • Grills, toasters and radiant heaters (e.g. electric fires) • Optical fibre communication
Visible light	• Morse code with torches, photography, fibre optics

Reflection

When a wave strikes a reflective surface it changes direction. This is called **reflection**.

The **normal line** is a construction line drawn **perpendicular** to the reflecting surface at the point of incidence. The normal line is used to calculate the angles of incidence and reflection.

Light Reflected by a Plane Mirror

Object
Incident ray (travelling towards mirror)

Normal

Eye
Reflected ray (travelling away from mirror)

i

r

Surface of plane mirror

Point of incidence

→ Light ray
i Angle of incidence
r Angle of reflection

The **angle of incidence** is equal to the **angle of reflection**.

When an object is viewed in a plane mirror the image formed is…

* **virtual** (i.e. on the opposite side of the mirror)
* **upright** (i.e. in the same orientation)
* **the same size** as the object
* **laterally inverted** (i.e. left becomes right)

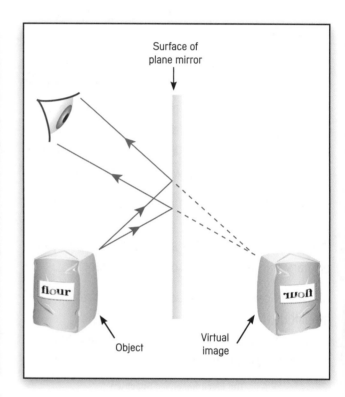

Surface of plane mirror

flour

flour

Object

Virtual image

Sound

Sound also travels as a wave. These are called **longitudinal waves** because they cause vibrations (backwards and forwards) within a material (medium). **Sound waves** can't travel through a vacuum.

The frequency of a **sound wave** is the number of vibrations produced every second, i.e. **hertz** (Hz). Humans can hear sounds in the range between 20Hz and 20 000Hz (20kHz).

The **pitch** of a sound is determined by its **frequency**. As the frequency increases the pitch becomes higher.

Echoes are examples of sound being **reflected** at a **surface**.

Red-shift

If a wave source (e.g. light, sound or microwaves) is moving away from, or towards, an observer, there will be a change in the...

- observed **wavelength**
- observed **frequency**.

The model that's used to describe this phenomenon is known as the **Doppler effect**. An ambulance racing past you is a good example of the Doppler effect with sound waves.

- When a light source moves **away** from you, the observed **wavelength increases** and the **frequency decreases**. This is known as red-shift.
- When a light source moves **towards** you, the observed **wavelength decreases** and the **frequency increases**. This is known as **blue-shift**.

The Big Bang

The observed red-shift of galaxies supports the idea that...

- the whole Universe is **expanding**
- the expansion began from a very small initial point in a huge explosion known as the **Big Bang**.

Cosmic Microwave Background Radiation (CMBR) is a form of electromagnetic radiation that fills the entire Universe. It comes from radiation that was around shortly after the beginning of the Universe but which has now been stretched.

The Big Bang theory is currently the **only theory** that can explain the existence of CMBR.

The light observed from distant **galaxies** in the Universe is **red-shifted**. In fact the further away a galaxy is, the faster it is moving and the bigger the observed increase in wavelength.

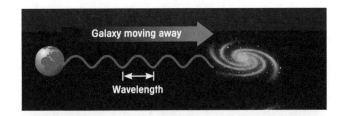

Galaxy moving away

Wavelength

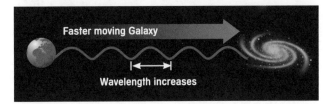

Faster moving Galaxy

Wavelength increases

Quick Test

1. Do radio waves and gamma rays travel through a vacuum (space) at the same speed?
2. What is the amplitude of a wave?
3. When an object is viewed in a plane mirror what does the image look like?
4. What type of wave is a sound wave?
5. Between what two frequencies can humans hear sound?
6. Give two pieces of evidence that the red-shift of light provides in terms of our Universe.

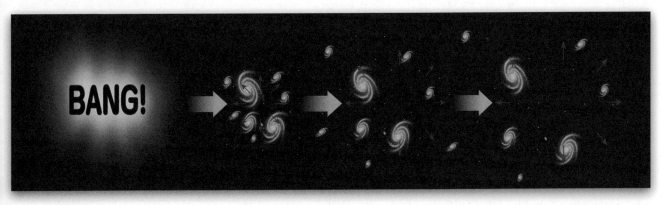

BANG!

1. Different materials require different amounts of energy to raise their temperature by 1°C. In fact the energy (E) required can be calculated using the equation:

$$E = m \times c \times \theta$$

(a) Explain the meanings of the symbols m, c and θ.

(3 marks)

(b) An electric kettle is used to boil some water.

The amount of water is 0.6kg, and room temperature is taken to be 20°C. If the specific heat capacity of the water is 4200J / kg°C, determine how much energy will be needed to raise the temperature of the water to its boiling point.

(2 marks)

(c) The power rating of a kettle is 1.7kW.
(i) Calculate how long it will take for the water to boil (to the nearest minute).

(2 marks)

(ii) What is this time in terms of decimal hours?

(1 mark)

(d) Using the information above, determine the amount of energy used in kilowatt-hours.

(2 marks)

(e) If the unit cost of electricity is 10p per kilowatt-hour, how much does it cost to boil the water in the kettle?

(1 mark)

2 Different parts of the electromagnetic spectrum are used for communication. For example, visible light is used for photography and Morse code with torches.

(a) From the list below link the type of radiation (**A**, **B** and **C**) with the mode of communication (**1**, **2** and **3**).

A Microwaves   **1** Optical fibre communication

B Radio waves   **2** Mobile phones

C Infrared   **3** TV

(3 marks)

(b) The electromagnetic spectrum is shown below with wavelengths shown in metres. On the spectrum label the positions of microwaves, radio waves and infrared using the letters **A**, **B** and **C** (as above).

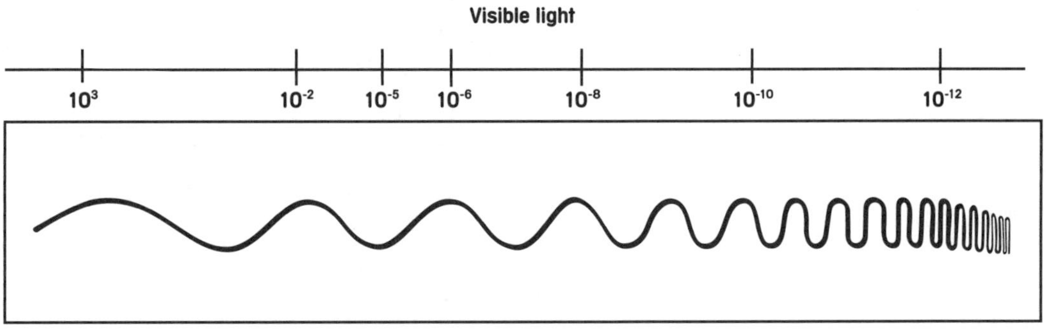

Visible light

| 10^3 | | 10^{-2} | 10^{-5} | 10^{-6} | | 10^{-8} | | 10^{-10} | | 10^{-12} |

(3 marks)

(c) Sound waves are also used in communication. Calculate the wavelength of a sound wave if the speed of sound in air is 330m/s and the frequency is 2000Hz.

(2 marks)

(d) Sound waves travel a lot faster in water than in the air; in fact approximately 1400m/s. Explain why sound waves travel faster in water.

(3 marks)

Answers

Biology

Quick Test Answers

Page 12
1. Professional athlete; PE teacher; office worker
2. Metabolic rate
3. Malnourished
4. Increase

Page 15
1. Viruses
2. Symptoms of a disease / illness
3. Semmelweiss
4. Antibodies
5. Resistant

Page 19
1. A synapse
2. A reflex action
3. a) Sensory neurone
   b) Glands and muscles (or the effector)
4. Enzymes work best at 37°C
5. Pituitary gland
6. LH

Page 20
1. Light, gravity and moisture
2. Auxin
3. Phototropism
4. Gravity
5. As a weed killer or rooting powder

Page 22
1. Drug
2. Placebo
3. It slows them down
4. Nicotine
5. They artificially enhance performance

Page 24
1. Light, space, water and nutrients from the soil
2. **Accept one from:** To prevent animals eating them; To reduce water loss through the leaves
3. **Accept any suitable answers, e.g.:** Camouflaged; Large surface area; Thick fur; Layer of insulating fat
4. A high level of air pollution
5. Organisms that live in extreme environments
6. Clean, oxygenated water
7. **Any one from:** Disease; Habitat loss; Climate change

Page 26
1. Warm, moist and plenty of oxygen
2. Respiration
3. **Any two from:** Heat loss; Waste (faeces); Movement
4. Biomass

Page 29
1. DNA
2. A gene
3. 23
4. Sexual reproduction
5. Clones
6. Embryo transplants
7. Special enzymes
8. **Any one from:** Effect on wildlife; Effect on human health

Page 31
1. Charles Darwin
2. **Accept any suitable answer, e.g.:** It challenged the idea that God made all the animals and plants that live on Earth; There was insufficient evidence to convince many scientists when it was published; The mechanism of inheritance and variation was not known until 50 years after the theory was published.
3. Jean-Baptiste Lamarck
4. Fossils
5. Mutation
6. Because of differences in their genes

Exam Practice Answers

Pages 32-33
1. a) The liver
   b) Your diet; Inherited factors
2. a) Small amounts of inactive / dead pathogen
   b) Antibodies
   c) Bacteria
3. a) $\dfrac{(5+5+6+7)}{4} = \dfrac{23}{4} = 5.75mm$
   b) Plate 4 (bathroom cleaner)
   c) As a control that the student could compare her results against
   d) By repeating her investigation four times
4. a) Sensory
   b) Effector (muscle or gland)
   c) Synapse
5. a) Follicle stimulating hormone (FSH)
   b) Oestrogen
   c) i) FSH and LH are given to help stimulate eggs to mature
      ii) Oestrogen or progesterone are given to prevent FSH production so eggs don't mature.
6. a) **Accept any suitable answer, e.g.:** Affects the nervous system, slowing down reactions; Helps people to relax; Can lead to lack of self control; Unconsciousness, coma or death; Can lead to liver damage or brain damage
   b) **Accept any suitable answer, e.g.:** Emphysema; Coughing; Bronchitis; Heart disease; Lung cancer
7. **Accept two from:** Small ears that help to reduce its surface area and heat loss; A thick insulating coat to help reduce heat loss; White coat for camouflage to help hide from predators and attack prey; Short legs so there is less surface area for heat loss; White fur so less heat loss due to radiated heat.

Chemistry

Quick Test Answers

Page 36
1. Protons and neutrons
2. The number of electrons in the highest energy level of an atom is the same as the group the element is in, e.g. all atoms in Group 2 have two electrons in the highest energy level. (Helium is the only exception).
3. 2,8,2

Page 39
1. Calcium oxide and carbon dioxide
2. Carbon dioxide turns limewater cloudy
3. (Powdered) clay
4. a) $4Al + 3O_2 \rightarrow 2Al_2O_3$
   b) $2Cr + 6HCl \rightarrow 2CrCl_3 + 3H_2$

Page 42
1. concentrated; purified
2. Carbon
3. Phytomining and bioleaching
4. A mixture of a metal with at least one other substance/element (e.g. carbon or another metal)
5. Because the layers of atoms are easily able to slide over each other
6. To strengthen them
7. Transition metals

Page 47
1. Carbon and hydrogen
2. Fractional distillation
3. **Any two from:** Carbon dioxide; Water (vapour); Carbon monoxide; Sulfur dioxide; Oxides of nitrogen
4. Acid rain and global warming
5. Cracking
6. Alkenes
7. Add bromine water; it turns from orange to colourless (is decolourised).
8. Monomers

Page 49
1. They provide energy and nutrients
2. Vegetable oils have a higher boiling point than water
3. **Any two from:** Salad dressings; Ice creams; Cosmetics; Paints
4. Double carbon–carbon bonds (C = C)

Page 51
1. a) mantle, crust
   b) move
   c) tectonic plates

Page 53
1. a) Nitrogen and oxygen
   b) **Any one from:** Carbon dioxide; Water vapour; Noble gases
2. By plants (photosynthesis)
3. In sedimentary rocks and by the oceans

Exam Practice Answers

Pages 54-55
1. a) Positive
   b) 11
   c)

   d) i) 3
      ii) $4Na + O_2 \rightarrow 2Na_2O$
2. a) Quarried / mined
   b) **Any one from:** Magnesium; Copper; Zinc; Calcium; Sodium
   c) Limewater turns milky (or cloudy)
3. a) It is a good conductor of electricity
   b) By heating the ore in a furnace (smelting)
   c) Electrolysis
   d) **Any one from:** Phytomining; Bioleaching
4. a) Two or more elements or compounds that are not chemically combined
   b) Carbon and hydrogen
   c) **Any one from:** Carbon dioxide; Carbon monoxide; Water vapour; Sulfur dioxide
   d) Cracking
5. a) X   b) Y   c) Y   d) Y

Answers

Quick Test Answers

Page 59
1. Infrared radiation
2. True
3. Regular or orderly pattern
4. The movement of fast-moving free electrons
5. **Any two from:** Amount of surface area of a material; A material's temperature; The air pressure
6. How effective a material is as an insulator
7. 42 000J

Page 61
1. It is wasted; Turns into heat; Warms the surroundings
2. 12.5%
3. An energy transfer diagram showing arrows that are proportional to the amount of energy involved in each process
4. **(a)** Joules or kilowatt-hours **(b)** watts or kilowatts
5. 200W
6. **(a)** 1.2kWh **(b)** 12p

Page 64
1. **Any two from:** Coal; Oil; Gas
2. Solid, liquid or gas obtained from lifeless or living biological material
3. **Advantages:** Free electricity; Lack of air pollution; Expensive to set up; Inefficient
   Disadvantages: Expensive; Inefficient
4. Prevents carbon dioxide build up in the atmosphere; Stored in old oil fields or gas fields
5. High voltage reduces current and hence minimises energy loss
6. Converts the potential difference on the overhead cables to a safe level of 230V for consumers, e.g. houses

Page 67
1. Yes
2. The maximum or minimum height (disturbance) of a wave from the midpoint.

3. Upright, same size, virtual and laterally inverted
4. Longitudinal
5. Between 20Hz and 20 000Hz
6. It is expanding; It started off from a very small initial point (Big Bang)

Exam Practice Answers

Pages 68-69
1. **a)** m is the mass (in kg); c is the specific thermal capacity (in J/kg°C), θ is the change in temperature (°C)
   b) $E = mc\theta = 0.6 \times 4200 \times (100 - 20)$
   $E = 201600J$ or $\approx 202kJ$ (*1 mark for correct substitution into equation and 1 mark for answer*)
   c) (i) Using $E = Pt$ and rearranging gives $t = \dfrac{E}{p} = \dfrac{201600}{1.7 \times 10^3} = 118.6s \approx 2$ min
   (*1 mark for correct substitution into equation and 1 mark for answer*)
   (ii) $t = \dfrac{2}{60} = 0.033$hrs
   d) $E = Pt = 1.7kW \times 0.033hrs; = 0.057kWh$
   e) Cost $= 0.057kWh \times 10p = 0.57p$
2. **a)** A 2; B 3; C 1
   b)

B		A	C			
10^3		10^{-2} 10^{-5}	10^{-6}	10^{-8}	10^{-10}	10^{-12}

   c) $v = f\lambda$ and hence $\lambda = \dfrac{v}{f}$; $= \dfrac{330}{2000} = 0.165m$
   d) Sound waves need a medium to travel in; Water molecules are closer together than air molecules; Sound waves are therefore transmitted through the material at a faster rate.

Biology

Adaptation – the gradual change of a particular organism over generations to become better suited to its environment

Aerobic – with oxygen

Antibiotic – medication used to kill bacterial pathogens inside the body

Antibody – a protein produced in the body by the immune system to kill particular pathogens

Asexual reproduction – when new individuals are produced that are identical to their parents; doesn't involve the fusion of gametes

Auxin – a growth hormone produced in plants

Bacteria – a single-celled microorganism that has no nucleus

Bias – where results are influenced unfairly by an individual's beliefs or opinions

Biomass – amount of biological matter; the mass of a plant or animal without the water content

Carbon cycle – the constant recycling of carbon through the processes in life, death and decay

Carcinogen – a substance that causes cancer

Cholesterol – a fatty substance that is found in all cells of the body

Chromosome – long molecule found in the nucleus of all cells; made from DNA

Clone – an offspring that is genetically identical to the parent organism

Communities – groups of species living in the same place

Culture medium – a substance that provides the nutrients for the artificial growth of bacteria and other cells

Decay – to rot or decompose

Deficiency disease – a disease caused by the lack of an essential element in the diet

Detritus – organic material from dead and decomposing plants and animals

DNA (deoxyribo nucleic acid) – nuclei acid molecules that contain genetic information and make up chromosomes

Drug – a chemical substance that alters the way the body works

Effector – part of the body (e.g. a muscle or a gland) that produces a response to a stimuli

Embryo – a ball of cells that will develop into a human / animal baby

Environment – the area and conditions in which an organism lives

Enzyme – a protein that speeds up a reaction (a biological catalyst)

Evolve – to change naturally over a period of time

Extinct – a species that has died out

Extremophile – an organism that can live in very extreme environments

Fertilisation – the fusion of the male and female gametes

Fetus – an unborn human / animal baby

Food chain – the feeding relationship between organisms

Fossil – the remains of animals / plants preserved in rock

FSH (follicle stimulating hormone) – a hormone that stimulates ovaries to produce oestrogen

Gamete – a specialised sex cell formed by meiosis

Gene – part of a chromosome made up of DNA; controls a certain characteristic

Genetic modification (GM) – organisms that have had specific areas of their genetic material changed using genetic engineering techniques

Gland – an organ in an animal's body that secretes substances, e.g. hormones

Gravitropism (or Geotropism) – a plant's growth response to gravity

Hormone – a regulatory substance that stimulates cells or tissues into action; produced by a gland

Incubated – to grow under conditions that encourage development, e.g. to grow microorganisms in a laboratory under controlled conditions

Infectious – a disease that is easily spread through air, water, etc.

Glossary

In vitro **fertilisation (IVF)** – a process where an egg is fertilised by sperm outside of the body

Leprosy – a contagious bacterial disease affecting the skin and nerves

LH (luteinising hormone) – a hormone that stimulates the release of an egg in the menstrual cycle

Malnourished – suffering from a lack of essential food nutrients

Menstrual cycle – the monthly cycle of hormonal changes in a woman

Metabolic rate – the rate at which an animal uses energy over a given time period

MRSA (Methicillin-resistant *Staphylococcus aureus*) – an antibiotic-resistant bacterium; a 'superbug'

Mutation – a spontaneous change in the genetic material of a cell

Natural selection – the survival of individual organisms that are best suited / adapted to their environment

Neurone – a specialised cell that transmits electrical messages or nerve impulses

Obesity – the condition of being very overweight

Oestrogen – a hormone secreted by the ovaries that inhibits the production of FSH and causes the production of LH

Pathogen – a disease-causing microorganism

Petri dish – a round, shallow dish used to grow bacteria

Photosynthesis – the chemical process that uses light energy to produce glucose in green plants

Phototropism – a plant's growth response to light

Pituitary gland – a small gland at the base of the brain that produces hormones

Placebo – a dummy drug given to patients during drug trials

Predator – an animal that hunts, kills and eats other animals (prey)

Radiation – electromagnetic particles / rays emitted by a radioactive substance

Receptor – cells found in sense organs, e.g. eyes, ears, nose

Reflex action – an involuntary action, e.g. automatically and very quickly removing your hand from something hot

Respiration – the process of converting glucose into energy inside cells

Semmelweiss – a doctor who recognised the importance of good hygiene in hospitals

Sexual reproduction – when new individuals are produced that aren't genetically identical to the parents; involving the fusion of gametes

Side effect – condition caused by taking medication, e.g. headache, nausea

Specialised – adapted for a particular purpose

Statin – a drug used to help lower cholesterol levels in the blood

Sterilisation – making something free from all microorganisms

Stimuli – change in an environment

Synapse – the gap between two neurones

Toxin – a poison produced by a living organism

Tropism – a growth in response to a stimulus, e.g. plants growing towards the light

Vaccine – a liquid preparation containing inactive or dead pathogens, used to make the body produce antibodies to provide protection against disease

Variation – differences between individuals of the same species

Chemistry

Alkane – a saturated hydrocarbon with the general formula C_nH_{2n+2}

Alkene – an unsaturated hydrocarbon (with at least one double carbon–carbon bond) with the general formula C_nH_{2n}

Alloy – a mixture of two or more metals, or a mixture of one metal and a non-metal

Atom – the smallest part of an element that can enter into a chemical reaction

Atomic number – the number of protons in an atom

Biodegradable – a substance that does decompose naturally

Biofuel – a fuel produced from plant material

Bioleaching – an extraction method that uses bacteria to extract metals from low-grade ores

Catalyst – a substance that increases the rate of a chemical reaction without being changed itself

Chemical formula – a way of showing the elements that are present in molecules of a substance

Chemical reaction – a process in which one or more substances are changed into others

Compound – a substance consisting of two or more elements chemically combined together

Conductor – a substance that readily transfers heat or energy

Cracking – the process used to break down long-chain hydrocarbons into more useful short-chain hydrocarbons, using high temperatures and a catalyst

Crude oil – a liquid mixture found in rocks that contains hydrocarbons

Decomposition – breaking down

Distillation – a process of separating a liquid mixture by boiling it and condensing its vapours

Electrolysis – the process by which an electric current causes a solution to undergo chemical decomposition

Electron – a negatively charged subatomic particle that orbits the nucleus

Element – a substance that consists of only one type of atom

Emulsion – a mixture of oil and water

Evidence – observations, measurements and data collected and subjected to some form of validation

Fermentation – the process by which yeast converts sugars to alcohol and carbon dioxide through anaerobic respiration

Fossil – the remains of animals / plants preserved in rock

Fossil fuel – fuel formed in the ground, over millions of years, from the remains of dead plants and animals

Fractional distillation – the process used to separate crude oil into groups of hydrocarbons whose molecules have a similar number of carbon atoms

Fuel – a substance that releases heat or energy when combined with oxygen

Global warming – the increase in the average temperature on Earth due to a rise in the levels of greenhouse gases in the atmosphere

Hydrocarbon – a compound containing only hydrogen and carbon

Mass number – the total number of protons and neutrons present in an atom

Mineral – a naturally occurring chemical element or compound found in rocks

Mixture – two or more elements or compounds that are not chemically combined

Neutron – a subatomic particle found in the nucleus of an atom that has no charge

Non-biodegradable – a substance that doesn't decompose naturally by the action of microorganisms

Nucleus – the small central core of an atom, consisting of protons and neutrons

Ore – a naturally occurring mineral, from which it is economically viable to extract

Phytomining – an extraction method that uses plants to extract copper

Pollution – the contamination of an environment by chemicals, waste or heat

Polymer – a giant, long-chained hydrocarbon

Polymerisation – the process of monomers joining together to form a polymer

Glossary

Product – a substance made at the end of a chemical reaction

Proton – a positively charged subatomic particle found in the nucleus

Reactant – a substance present before a chemical reaction takes place

Saturated (hydrocarbon) – a hydrocarbon molecule with no double bonds

Sedimentary rock – rock formed by the accumulation of sediment

Smelting – a method of extracting a metal from its ore by heating the ore in a furnace

Tectonic plates – huge sections of the Earth's crust that move in relation to one another

Theory – the best way to explain why something is happening. It can be changed when new evidence is found

Thermal decomposition – the breakdown of a chemical substance due to the action of heat

Unsaturated – a term used to describe alkenes that identifies the presence of a C=C bond

HT **Emulsifier** – a substance that helps to stabilise an emulsion

Hydrogenation – the process in which hydrogen is used to harden vegetable oils

Hydrophilic – water-loving molecule

Hydrophobic – water-hating molecule

Physics

Amplitude – the maximum disturbance/vibration measured from midpoint

Big Bang – the massive explosion that sent all matter outwards signalling the start of the Universe creating space and time

Biofuel – a solid, liquid or gas obtained from lifeless or living biological material

Condensation – the change of a vapour into a liquid accompanied by heat transfer

Conduction – the energy transfer in solids without the substance itself moving

Conductor – a material that readily transfers energy by atom vibration or electrical energy through the movement of free electrons

Convection – the energy transfer through movement in liquids and gases

Cosmic Microwave Background Radiation (CMBR) – electromagnetic radiation that fills the entire Universe; remnant of the Big Bang

Doppler effect – the change in wavelength or frequency associated with a moving source

Echo – a reflected sound wave

Efficiency – the ratio of energy (useful power) output to total energy (power) input, expressed as a percentage or as a decimal number

Electrical energy – energy of electrical charge or current; measured in joules (J)

Energy transfer – a measure of how much work is done on an object or material

Evaporation – the change from liquid into a vapour below the boiling point of the liquid

Fossil fuel – a fuel formed in the ground over millions of years from the remains of dead plants and animals

Frequency – the number of cycles or oscillations that occur in 1 second; measured in hertz (Hz)

Infrared radiation – the transfer of thermal radiation by electromagnetic waves

Insulator – a material that doesn't conduct well

Kinetic theory – a theory that explains the physical properties of matter in terms of the movement of particles

Longitudinal wave – a wave where the oscillations are parallel to the direction of energy transfer

National Grid – a network of power lines and cables that carries electricity from the power station to the consumer

Non-renewable energy source – an energy source that can't be replaced as fast as it is used

Normal line – the line constructed at 90° to the reflecting surface at the point of incidence

Nuclear fuels – uranium and plutonium used in nuclear power stations to provide the transfer of energy by heat

Potential difference – the energy transfer by unit charge passing from one point to another; measured in volts (V)

Power – work done or energy transferred in a given time; units of watts (W); $P = \frac{E}{T}$ and $P = I \times V$

Red-shift – the shift in light or other electromagnetic waves to longer wavelengths

Reflection – a change in direction of a wave when striking a plane surface

Renewable energy source – an energy source that can be replaced faster than it is used

Sankey diagram – an energy transfer diagram where the widths of the arrows are proportional to the amount of energy used

Sound wave – forward and backward vibrations within a material or medium; sound waves are longitudinal waves; can't travel through a vacuum

Specific heat capacity – the amount of energy required to change the temperature of 1kg of a material by 1°C; measured in J/kg°C

Thermal radiation – the transfer of infrared radiation; does not involve particles

Transformer – an electrical device used to change the voltage or potential difference of alternating currents

Transverse wave – a wave where the oscillations are perpendicular to the direction of energy transfer

U-value – a measure of the effectiveness of a material as an insulator

Wave equation – an equation that connects frequency and wavelength for waves; $v = f \times \lambda$

Wavelength – the distance between two successive peaks or troughs in a wave

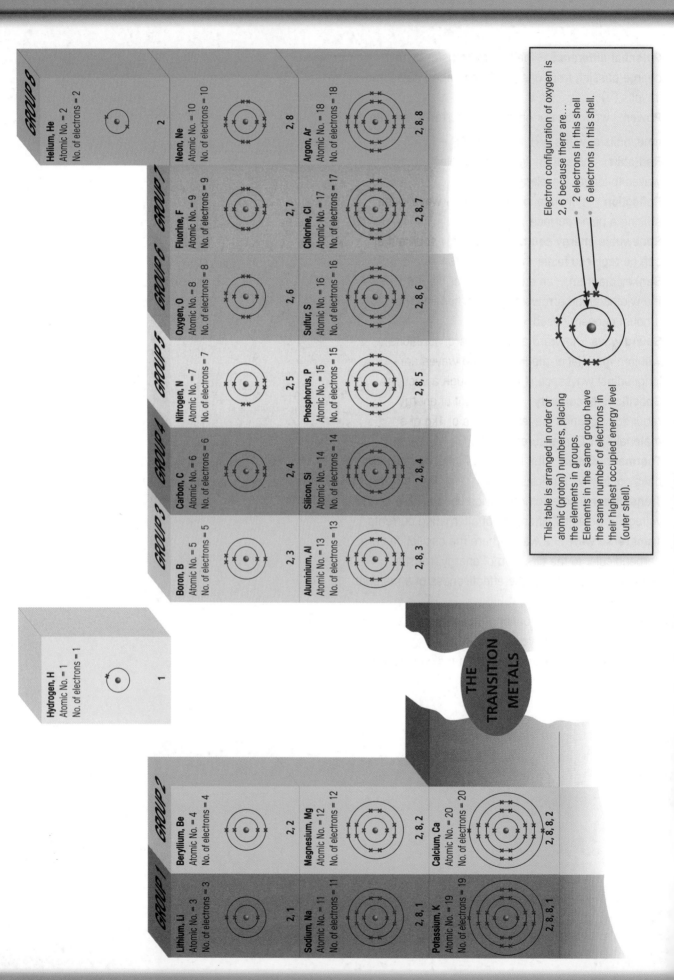

GROUP 8

Helium, He
Atomic No. = 2
No. of electrons = 2

2

Neon, Ne
Atomic No. = 10
No. of electrons = 10

2, 8

Argon, Ar
Atomic No. = 18
No. of electrons = 18

2, 8, 8

GROUP 7

Fluorine, F
Atomic No. = 9
No. of electrons = 9

2, 7

Chlorine, Cl
Atomic No. = 17
No. of electrons = 17

2, 8, 7

GROUP 6

Oxygen, O
Atomic No. = 8
No. of electrons = 8

2, 6

Sulfur, S
Atomic No. = 16
No. of electrons = 16

2, 8, 6

GROUP 5

Nitrogen, N
Atomic No. = 7
No. of electrons = 7

2, 5

Phosphorus, P
Atomic No. = 15
No. of electrons = 15

2, 8, 5

GROUP 4

Carbon, C
Atomic No. = 6
No. of electrons = 6

2, 4

Silicon, Si
Atomic No. = 14
No. of electrons = 14

2, 8, 4

GROUP 3

Boron, B
Atomic No. = 5
No. of electrons = 5

2, 3

Aluminium, Al
Atomic No. = 13
No. of electrons = 13

2, 8, 3

Hydrogen, H
Atomic No. = 1
No. of electrons = 1

1

THE TRANSITION METALS

GROUP 1

Lithium, Li
Atomic No. = 3
No. of electrons = 3

2, 1

Sodium, Na
Atomic No. = 11
No. of electrons = 11

2, 8, 1

Potassium, K
Atomic No. = 19
No. of electrons = 19

2, 8, 8, 1

GROUP 2

Beryllium, Be
Atomic No. = 4
No. of electrons = 4

2, 2

Magnesium, Mg
Atomic No. = 12
No. of electrons = 12

2, 8, 2

Calcium, Ca
Atomic No. = 20
No. of electrons = 20

2, 8, 8, 2

This table is arranged in order of atomic (proton) numbers, placing the elements in groups.
Elements in the same group have the same number of electrons in their highest occupied energy level (outer shell).

Electron configuration of oxygen is 2, 6 because there are...
• 2 electrons in this shell
• 6 electrons in this shell.

Key

relative atomic mass
atomic symbol
name
atomic (proton) number

1	2											3	4	5	6	7	0
							1 **H** hydrogen 1										4 **He** helium 2
7 **Li** lithium 3	9 **Be** beryllium 4											11 **B** boron 5	12 **C** carbon 6	14 **N** nitrogen 7	16 **O** oxygen 8	19 **F** fluorine 9	20 **Ne** neon 10
23 **Na** sodium 11	24 **Mg** magnesium 12											27 **Al** aluminium 13	28 **Si** silicon 14	31 **P** phosphorus 15	32 **S** sulfur 16	35.5 **Cl** chlorine 17	40 **Ar** argon 18
39 **K** potassium 19	40 **Ca** calcium 20	45 **Sc** scandium 21	48 **Ti** titanium 22	51 **V** vanadium 23	52 **Cr** chromium 24	55 **Mn** manganese 25	56 **Fe** iron 26	59 **Co** cobalt 27	59 **Ni** nickel 28	63.5 **Cu** copper 29	65 **Zn** zinc 30	70 **Ga** gallium 31	73 **Ge** germanium 32	75 **As** arsenic 33	79 **Se** selenium 34	80 **Br** bromine 35	84 **Kr** krypton 36
85 **Rb** rubidium 37	88 **Sr** strontium 38	89 **Y** yttrium 39	91 **Zr** zirconium 40	93 **Nb** niobium 41	96 **Mo** molybdenum 42	[98] **Tc** technetium 43	101 **Ru** ruthenium 44	103 **Rh** rhodium 45	106 **Pd** palladium 46	108 **Ag** silver 47	112 **Cd** cadmium 48	115 **In** indium 49	119 **Sn** tin 50	122 **Sb** antimony 51	128 **Te** tellurium 52	127 **I** iodine 53	131 **Xe** xenon 54
133 **Cs** caesium 55	137 **Ba** barium 56	139 **La*** lanthanum 57	178 **Hf** hafnium 72	181 **Ta** tantalum 73	184 **W** tungsten 74	186 **Re** rhenium 75	190 **Os** osmium 76	192 **Ir** iridium 77	195 **Pt** platinum 78	197 **Au** gold 79	201 **Hg** mercury 80	204 **Tl** thallium 81	207 **Pb** lead 82	209 **Bi** bismuth 83	[209] **Po** polonium 84	[210] **At** astatine 85	[222] **Rn** radon 86
[223] **Fr** francium 87	[226] **Ra** radium 88	[227] **Ac*** actinium 89	[261] **Rf** rutherfordium 104	[262] **Db** dubnium 105	[266] **Sg** seaborgium 106	[264] **Bh** bohrium 107	[277] **Hs** hassium 108	[268] **Mt** meitnerium 109	[271] **Ds** darmstadtium 110	[272] **Rg** roentgenium 111							

Elements with atomic numbers 112–116 have been reported but not fully authenticated

*The Lanthanides (atomic numbers 58–71) and the Actinides (atomic numbers 90–103) have been omitted.

Cu and **Cl** have not been rounded to the nearest whole number.

Index